Lab Manual

AGS Publishing
Circle Pines, MN 55014-1796
800-328-2560

©2006 AGS Publishing
4201 Woodland Road
Circle Pines, MN 55014-1796
800-328-2560 • www.agsnet.com

AGS Publishing is a trademark and trade name of American Guidance Service, Inc.

Printed in the United States of America

ISBN 0-7854-3979-X

Product Number 94191

A 0 9 8 7 6 5 4 3 2 1

Table of Contents

Table of Contents, continued

Table of Contents, continued

Safety Rules and Symbols

In this book, you will learn about biology through investigations and labs. During these activities, it is important to follow safety rules, procedures, and your teacher's directions. You can avoid accidents by following directions and handling materials carefully. Read and follow the safety rules below, and learn the safety symbols. To alert you to possible dangers, safety symbols will appear with each investigation or lab. Reread the rules below often and review what the symbols mean.

General Safety

◆ Read each Express Lab, Investigation, and Discovery Investigation before doing it. Review the materials list and follow the safety symbols and safety alerts.

◆ Ask questions if you do not understand something.

◆ Never perform an experiment, mix substances, or use equipment without permission.

◆ Keep your work area clean and free of clutter.

◆ Be aware of other students working near you.

◆ Do not play or run during a lab activity. Take your lab work seriously.

◆ Know where fire extinguishers, fire alarms, first aid kits, fire blankets, and the nearest telephone are located. Be familiar with the emergency exits and evacuation route from your room.

◆ Keep your hands away from your face.

◆ Immediately report all accidents to your teacher, including injuries, broken equipment, and spills.

Flame/Heat Safety

◆ Clear your work space of materials that could burn or melt.

◆ Before using a burner, know how to operate the burner and gas outlet.

◆ Be aware of all open flames. Never reach across a flame.

◆ Never leave a flame or operating hot plate unattended.

◆ Do not heat a liquid in a closed container.

◆ When heating a substance in a test tube or flask, point the container away from yourself and others.

◆ Do not touch hot glassware or the surface of an operating hot plate or lightbulb.

◆ In the event of a fire, tell your teacher and leave the room immediately.

◆ If your clothes catch on fire, stop, drop to the floor, and roll.

Safety Rules and Symbols, continued

Electrical Safety

- Never use electrical equipment near water, on wet surfaces, or with wet hands or clothing.
- Alert your teacher to any frayed or damaged cords or plugs.
- Before plugging in equipment, be sure the power control is in the "off" position.
- Do not place electrical cords in walkways or let cords hang over table edges.
- Electricity flowing in wire causes the wire to become hot. Use caution.
- Turn off and unplug electrical equipment when you are finished using it.

Chemical Safety

- Check labels on containers to be sure you are using the right substance.
- Do not directly smell any substance. If you are instructed to smell a substance, gently fan your hand over the substance, waving its vapors toward you.
- When handling substances that give off gases or vapors, work in a fume hood or well-ventilated area.
- Do not taste any substance. Never eat, drink, or chew gum in your work area.
- Do not return unused chemicals to their original containers.
- Avoid skin contact with chemicals. Some chemicals can irritate or harm skin.
- If a chemical spills on your clothing or skin, rinse the area immediately with plenty of water. Tell your teacher.
- When diluting an acid or base with water, always add the acid or base to the water. Do not add water to the acid or base.
- Wash your hands after working with chemicals.

Eye Protection

- Wear safety goggles at all times or as directed by your teacher.
- If a chemical gets in your eyes or on your face, use an eyewash station or flush your eyes and face with running water immediately. Tell your teacher.

Animal Safety

- Do not touch or approach an animal without your teacher's permission.
- Handle and care for animals only as your teacher directs.
- If you are bitten, stung, or scratched by an animal, tell your teacher.
- Do not expose animals to loud noises, overcrowding, or other stresses.
- Wash your hands after touching an animal.

Safety Rules and Symbols, continued

Hand Safety

◆ Wear protective gloves when working with chemicals or solutions. Wear gloves for handling preserved specimens and plants.

◆ Do not touch an object that could be hot.

◆ Use tongs or utensils to hold a container over a heat source.

◆ Wash your hands when you are finished with a lab activity.

Plant Safety

◆ Do not place any part of a plant in your mouth. Do not rub plant parts or liquids on your skin.

◆ Wear gloves when handling plants or as directed by your teacher.

◆ Wash your hands after handling any part of a plant.

Glassware Safety

◆ Check glassware for cracks or chips before use. Give broken glassware to your teacher; do not use it.

◆ Keep glassware away from the edge of a work surface.

◆ If glassware breaks, tell your teacher. Dispose of glass according to your teacher's directions.

Clothing Protection

◆ Wear a lab coat or apron at all times or as directed by your teacher.

◆ Tie back long hair, remove dangling jewelry, and secure loose-fitting clothing.

◆ Do not wear open-toed shoes, sandals, or canvas shoes in the lab.

Sharp Object Safety

◆ Take care when using scissors, pins, scalpels, or pointed tools or blades.

◆ Cut objects on a suitable work surface. Cut away from yourself and others.

◆ If you cut yourself, notify your teacher.

Cleanup/Waste Disposal

◆ If a chemical spills, alert your teacher and ask for clean up instructions.

◆ Follow your teacher's directions to dispose and clean up substances.

◆ Turn off burners, water faucets, electrical equipment, and gas outlets.

◆ Clean equipment if needed and return it to its proper location.

◆ Clean your work area and work surface.

◆ Wash your hands when you are finished.

Express Lab 1

Use with Express Lab 1, page 5

Materials   safety goggles
solar cell with small connecting motor

Procedure

1. On a sunny day, take the solar cell and connecting motor outside. Put on safety goggles.

2. Observe the activity of the motor when the solar cell is exposed to the sun.

3. Cover the solar cell and observe the activity of the motor.

4. Uncover and cover the solar cell 2 or 3 times. Observe the activity of the motor.

Analysis

1. What was the source of energy in this activity?

_____

2. Why did the activity of the motor change when you covered the solar cell?

_____

_____

3. Describe the different ways that energy was transformed during this activity.

_____

_____

_____

Cycles of Energy

Energy cycles through ecosystems. Plants capture the energy of the sun and use it to make food. When plants die, their bodies break down and decay. Worms, fungi, and bacteria eat the decaying plant matter and use it as a source of energy. In this way, the energy of the sun travels through an ecosystem.

Materials   safety goggles
lab coat or apron
one 1-gallon or 2-gallon fish bowl
4 cups of garden soil (from a garden supply store)
1 sheet of notebook paper
3–5 earthworms (from a bait and tackle shop)
1 dead plant or dead plant parts (soft plant parts like leaves or fruits instead of stems)
$\frac{1}{4}$ cup of water

Procedure

1. Put on safety goggles and a lab coat or apron.

2. Place 4 cups of garden soil in the bottom of the fish bowl. Add dead plant or dead plant parts.

3. Tear the sheet of notebook paper into little pieces. Stir these pieces of paper into the soil.

4. Add enough water to the soil to moisten it but not enough to create puddles.

5. Gently transfer 3–5 earthworms into the soil mixture. **Safety Alert: Handle earthworms as little as possible and with care.**

6. You have created a mini-ecosystem. Place your mini-ecosystem in a place that does not receive direct sunlight.

7. Check on your mini-ecosystem every day for the next two weeks. If the soil gets dry, water it until it is damp, but not soggy.

Cleanup/Disposal

Follow your teacher's instructions for cleanup and disposal of materials.

Cycles of Energy, continued

Analysis

1. Worms eat dead plant and animal matter. What did your worms eat for
the two weeks of the experiment?

_____

2. What are the living things in this mini-ecosystem? What are the nonliving things?

_____

_____

3. What changes occurred in the mini-ecosystem over the two-week period?

_____

_____

Conclusions

1. Explain how the growth cycle and the ecological cycle are related.

_____

_____

2. Explain this statement: When you eat a hamburger, you are eating the sun's energy.

_____

_____

Explore Further

Create a mini-pond ecosystem using an aquarium or large jar, water, a gold fish, and
water plants. Compare the way energy cycles through a mini-pond ecosystem to
the way it cycles through the mini-ecosystem of land plants and animals.

_____

_____

_____

_____

What Is Life?

Use with Investigation 1, pages 15–16

Biologists study all kinds of life. Life takes on many diverse forms. All life runs through cycles of energy, growth, evolution, and ecology. In this lab, you will examine some different forms of life and note their different cycles.

Materials   safety goggles   petri dish with bacteria culture
                lab coat or apron   plant seeds
                houseplant   plant sprout
                insect in a jar   rock
                mushroom in a plastic bag flashlight

Procedure

1. To record your data, make a data table like the one shown here.

Sample	Energy Cycle	Growth Cycle	Evolutionary Cycle	Ecological Cycle	Living/ Nonliving
1					
2					
3					
4					
5					
6					
7					
8					

2. Put on safety goggles and lab coat or apron. **Safety Alert: Do not open containers or touch specimens unless your teacher directs you to do so.**

3. Examine each sample. Use a flashlight if needed. Make a check mark in the Energy Cycle column if you think the sample is involved in an energy cycle.

What Is Life?, continued

4. Repeat Step 3 for each cycle. Place a check mark in the column if you think the sample is involved in that cycle.

5. In the final column, decide whether the sample is living or nonliving.

Cleanup/Disposal

Follow your teacher's instructions for disposal of any samples.

Analysis

1. Which samples are living and which are nonliving?

   _____

   _____

2. Which nonliving samples show some cycles that are common with cycles of living samples? What are the cycles?

   _____

   _____

   _____

Conclusions

1. What forms does energy take while cycling between living things? Describe two examples.

   _____

   _____

2. Which living samples are a part of the cycles of other living samples?

   _____

   _____

Explore Further

Think of two or more organisms that are part of a cycle. Create a diagram showing the organisms in the cycle. Label your diagram with the cycle's name.

No More Music

Jody is in her room, listening to her favorite new CD. She uses her CD player all the time and takes it with her everywhere. She is enjoying the music. Suddenly the music stops. Oh, no! She just got this CD last week. How could this happen? In this lab, you will use the scientific method to solve Jody's problem.

Materials   pencil
science notebook

Procedure

1. Use the data table below to record your data. In column 1, list the six steps of the scientific method: Observation, Question, Hypothesis, Experiment, Analysis, and Communication.

2. In column 2 next to Observation, write what you already know about Jody and her CD player.

3. In column 2 next to Question, write a question that expresses what you want to find out.

4. In column 2 next to Hypothesis, write your best guess about what happened to Jody's CD player.

5. In column 2 next to Experiment, write a way to test your hypothesis.

6. Assume that your experiment fixed Jody's CD player. In column 2 next to Analysis, record the conclusions you can make based on your experiment.

7. In column 2 next to Communication, suggest ways to share this information with others.

Steps of the Scientific Method	Your Data
1.	
2.	
3.	
4.	
5.	
6.	

No More Music, continued

Cleanup/Disposal

Follow your teacher's instructions for cleanup and disposal of materials.

Analysis

1. If your experiment had proved your hypothesis to be wrong, what could you have done next?

_____

2. Why do scientists share experimental results?

_____

3. Why would Jody want to share her results with her friends?

_____

Conclusions

1. Why is the scientific method a good way to solve problems?

_____

2. Who are some of the people that use the scientific method every day?

_____

Explore Further

How could you use the scientific method to find out whether brand X gasoline provides better gas mileage than brand Y?

_____

_____

_____

Using the Scientific Method

Use with Discovery Investigation 1, pages 23–24

Scientists answer questions and solve problems in an orderly way. They use a series of steps called the scientific method. How can you use the scientific method to answer questions? You will find out in this lab.

Suppose you are watching a news report about acid rain. The report explains that acid rain is rain that has more acid in it than usual. The acid forms from certain kinds of air pollution. The report shows trees that have been damaged by acid rain. You wonder: How might acid rain affect the way a plant starts growing?

Materials
safety goggles
lab coat or apron
2 clear plastic cups

20 corn seeds
water
vinegar

paper towels
eyedropper

Procedure

1. In a small group, discuss the question in the second paragraph above. Then write a hypothesis about how acid rain might affect the way a plant starts growing. The hypothesis should be one that you could test with an experiment.

   Hypothesis: _____

2. Write a procedure for your experiment. Number the steps. Include any Safety Alerts.

   _____

   _____

   _____

3. Be sure your experiment changes only one variable, or factor, at a time. Include a control group. Remember that a control is a setup for which you do not change any variables.

4. Draw a data table to record your data for 8 days.

5. Have your hypothesis, procedure, and Safety Alerts approved by your teacher. Then carry out your experiment.

Cleanup/Disposal

Before leaving the lab, clean up your materials and wash your hands.

Using the Scientific Method, continued

Analysis

1. What variable did you change in this experiment? _____

_____

2. What changes did you see among the corn seeds after Day 4? What changes

did you see after Day 8? _____

_____

_____

Conclusions

1. Was your hypothesis supported by the results of your investigation?

_____

2. What problems did you have in performing the experiment? What part of
the procedure would you change to be more successful?

_____

_____

_____

3. If a hypothesis is not supported by data from an experiment, is that experiment

a failure? Explain your answer. _____

_____

4. How do you think acid rain affects the way plants start growing?

_____

_____

Explore Further

In your group, discuss other variables that might affect how a plant starts
growing. Pick one question your group would like to investigate. Using the
scientific method, write a procedure to carry out your investigation.

_____

_____

_____

Express Lab 2

Use with Express Lab 2, page 33

Materials   safety goggles
lab coat or apron
2 clear plastic cups
plastic spoon
baking soda
water
measuring cup
vinegar

Procedure

1. Put on safety goggles and a lab coat or apron.

2. Put one level spoonful of baking soda into each plastic cup.
   Safety Alert: Do not taste or touch any chemicals.

3. Pour $\frac{1}{4}$ cup of water into one cup.

4. Pour $\frac{1}{4}$ cup of vinegar into the second cup.

5. Observe what happens in each cup.

Analysis

1. What happened in each cup?

   _____

   _____

2. In which cup is a chemical change happening?

   _____

   _____

Physical and Chemical Properties

Use with Investigation 2, pages 36–37

Matter has both physical and chemical properties. A change that does not affect the chemical makeup of a substance is a physical change. A chemical change involves a chemical reaction that changes the substance itself.

Materials

safety goggles	rusty nail	magnet
lab coat or apron	non-rusty nail	balance
flask	2 paper clips	crucible
water	hammer	magnesium strip
hot plate		

Procedure

1. Put on safety goggles and a lab coat or apron.

2. Fill a flask two-thirds full with water. Place the flask of water on a hot plate. Turn the plate on high. Observe what happens to the water as it boils. Turn off the hot plate.

3. Observe the rusty nail. Compare it to a non-rusty nail.

4. With a hammer, straighten a paper clip. Rub this paper clip with the magnet in the same direction about 30 times. Place this paper clip near another paper clip. Observe what happens.

5. Find the mass of the empty crucible and the strip of magnesium.

6. Ask your teacher to ignite the magnesium strip. Let it burn inside the crucible. **Safety Alert: Do not handle or move the crucible while the magnesium burns.**

7. Observe the burnt magnesium. Find the mass of the magnesium ashes and crucible.

Cleanup/Disposal

Follow your teacher's instructions to dispose of the rusty nail and burnt magnesium.

Analysis

1. What happened to the water as it boiled? Was this a physical change or a chemical change?

_____

_____

Physical and Chemical Properties, continued

2. What happened to the nail as it rusted? Was this a physical change or a chemical change?

_____

_____

3. What happened to the paper clip in Step 4? Was this a physical change or

a chemical change? _____

_____

4. Compare the mass of the magnesium strip to the magnesium ashes.

_____

_____

5. Did you watch a physical or chemical change in Step 6? Explain your answer.

_____

_____

Conclusions

1. Write a summary sentence for each of the four changes you observed. Explain

what changes took place. _____

_____

_____

_____

2. Why do you think there was a change in the mass of the magnesium after it burned?

What happens to a substance when it burns? _____

_____

_____

Explore Further

Look for evidence of three physical and three chemical changes in the environment
around you. Describe these changes in a list or paragraph.

_____

_____

Atomic Model

Everything is made up of tiny units of matter called atoms. Atoms are so small that one million of them lined up end to end would only equal the thickness of a hair. Even though no one has ever seen an atom, research shows that atoms contain three subatomic particles: protons, neutrons, and electrons. The protons and neutrons have about the same mass and are located inside the nucleus. Protons have a positive charge and neutrons are neutral. Electrons are tiny negatively charged particles that orbit the nucleus.

Very simple models of atoms are shown throughout Chapter 2. A helium atom is pictured on page 39, a sodium atom on page 48, and an oxygen atom and hydrogen atoms on page 53. In some of the drawings, the number of neutrons is not indicated. However, you can find the number of neutrons in an atom by subtracting the atomic number from the atomic mass.

The orbits of electrons are not very close to an atom's nucleus. In the lab, it is difficult to represent the distance between the nucleus of an element and the electrons of that element because it is so great. If a nucleus of a hydrogen atom were the size of a pencil eraser, the electrons orbiting would be about one-half mile (0.8 km) away!

Materials   safety goggles   paper plates
                        lab coat or apron   toothpicks
                        gum drops (in a variety of colors)   skewers
                        small marshmallows (in a variety of colors)   glue
                        clay or Playdough (in a variety of colors)   tape
                                                                scissors

Procedure

1. Put on safety goggles and a lab coat or apron.

2. Look over the list of materials provided for this lab.

3. Your job is to create a model of an atom using the materials available. You do not have to use all of the materials. You can make your model of any atom of the Periodic Table.

4. Your model should include the appropriate number of protons, neutrons, and electrons.

5. On a piece of paper, create a key for your model. A key explains what each part of a model represents. For example, if you use pink marshmallows to represent protons, glue a pink marshmallow on a piece of paper and label it "proton." Do the same for the other parts of the atom.

Cleanup/Disposal

Follow your teacher's instructions for cleanup and disposal of materials.

Atomic Model, continued

Analysis

Protons and neutrons are located in the nuclei of atoms. The number of protons is represented by the atomic number. The atomic mass represents the number of protons and neutrons. Atoms that are electrically neutral have the same number of protons and neutrons. Use the Periodic Table to complete the following table.

Atoms	Atomic Mass	Atomic Number	Number Protons	Number of Neutrons	Number of Electrons
hydrogen (H)					
lithium (Li)					
nitrogen (N)					
sodium (Na)					

Conclusions

1. All matter is made up of atoms. Would it be true or false to say that all matter is made up of protons, neutrons, and electrons? Explain you answer.

_____

_____

2. As you move from the left side of the Periodic Table to the right side, would you expect models of atoms to increase in size or decrease in size? Explain your answer.

_____

_____

Explore Further

In the air, oxygen does not exist as single atoms. Two atoms of oxygen pair to form molecules of O_2. In O_2, the oxygen atoms share electrons in the outer electron shells. Create a model of an O_2 molecule. Write a description of your model.

_____

_____

_____

_____

The Properties of Water

Use with Discovery Investigation 2, pages 57–58

Life on Earth owes much to the unique properties of water. These properties include water's ability to resist temperature change, create surface tension, expand as it freezes, and dissolve certain substances. In this lab, you will pick one property of water and develop a procedure to test it.

Materials			
safety goggles	sugar	heat lamp	plastic water bottle
lab coat or apron	salt	eyedropper	freezer
clear plastic cups	spoon	pipette	hot plate
sand	thermometers	vegetable oil	paper towels
water			

Procedure

1. Choose one of the following properties of water:
   - It holds heat and resists temperature change.
   - Its molecules stick together, creating surface tension.
   - It expands as it changes from liquid to solid form.
   - It is an excellent solvent.

2. Ask a question about the property you have chosen. For example, if you chose that water is an excellent solvent, you could question which substances it will or will not dissolve. Write a hypothesis.

Hypothesis: _____

_____

3. Write a procedure that will demonstrate the property you chose. Include Safety Alerts.

_____

_____

_____

_____

4. Choose the materials you need from the materials listed. Or, create your own materials list. Include your materials list in your lab report.

5. Ask your teacher to approve your hypothesis, procedure, and Safety Alerts. Then obtain the materials you need and perform your procedure.

The Properties of Water, continued

Cleanup/Disposal

Before you leave the lab, be sure your work area is clean.

Analysis

1. Present your data so that someone who did not see your experiment can evaluate it.

2. If your experiment did not support your hypothesis or was otherwise unsuccessful, evaluate your procedure for problems. Write a new procedure to correct these problems.

_____

_____

Conclusions

1. How did your data answer the question you asked in Step 2 about the property of water?

_____

_____

2. What makes this property important to life? What would be the consequences of losing this property?

_____

_____

_____

3. What causes this property of water?

_____

_____

Explore Further

Choose another property for water from the list. Write a procedure to test it. Include the type of observations and data you would collect.

_____

_____

_____

_____

Acids and Bases

Acids and bases are chemicals that can be found in every part of life, even in the human body. Blood is slightly basic, with a pH of 7.4. Stomach acid is a strong acid with a pH around 2.

Many of the materials that you use every day are acids and bases. In the kitchen, cola, orange juice, and coffee are mild acids. Baking soda is a mild base. Most household cleaners are mild to moderate bases, while oven cleaners are strong bases.

In this lab, you will test the pH of household items. You will use hydronium test paper to find the pH of each item.

Materials

safety goggles
lab coat or apron
8 pieces of hydronium test paper
color chart of changes to
  hydronium test paper
cotton swabs or small pipettes
paper towels
window cleaner (a few drops)
shampoo

cola
coffee
vinegar
lemon juice
antacid dissolved in $\frac{1}{4}$ cup water
baking soda dissolved in $\frac{1}{4}$ cup water
sheet of notebook paper
tape

Procedure

1. Put on safety goggles and a lab coat or apron. **Safety Alerts: Take special care when working with acids and bases. If any gets on the skin or in the eye, rinse immediately with water.**

2. Place a piece of notebook paper on your desk.

3. Arrange strips of hydronium paper on the notebook paper. Leave an inch or more of space around each one. Secure each piece in place with a small strip of tape.

4. Below each piece of paper, write the name of the material you plan to test. Label the strips as window cleaner, shampoo, cola, coffee, vinegar, antacid, and baking soda.

5. Collect a drop of window cleaner in a pipette or swab. Transfer the drop to the first piece of hydronium paper. Note the color change. Compare the new color of the hydronium paper to the colors on the color chart. Record the pH of the window cleaner in the data table.

Acids and Bases, continued

Household Item	Amount of pH	Household Item	Amount of pH
window cleaner		vinegar	
shampoo		lemon juice	
cola		antacid	
coffee		baking soda	

Cleanup/Disposal

Follow your teacher's instructions for cleanup and disposal of materials.

Analysis

1. How many of the items you tested were acids? _____ How many were bases? _____

2. Are you more likely to find acids in the kitchen or among the cleaning supplies? _____

3. Based on the findings in today's lab, if you were asked to predict the pH of each of the following, what would you say? Write your pH prediction on the line next to each item in the list.

_____ bath soap   _____ apple juice

_____ laundry detergent   _____ a cup of hot tea

_____ oven cleaner

Conclusions

1. In general, in what part of the home do you find the most acids? Where do you find

   the most bases? _____

   _____

2. Describe what life might be like if there were no acids and bases, and everything had a pH of 7.

   _____

   _____

Explore Further

Test the pH of some materials around the school. Stir a little chalk dust in water and test it. Find out what kind of cleaning solution the custodians use at your school and test that. Test the pH of some items from the lunchroom. Create a data table to record your results.

Studying Dehydration Synthesis

All organic compounds contain carbon (C), and many also contain oxygen (O) and hydrogen (H). Many of the organic compounds are made of long chains of smaller units. For example, a carbohydrate is made up of a chain of glucose molecules. Two glucose molecules combine in a process called dehydration synthesis. During this process, water molecules are formed as by-products.

Materials   safety goggles   scissors
                     lab apron or lab coat   tape
                     Figure A   notebook paper

Procedure

1. Put on safety goggles and a lab coat or apron.

2. Trace the three glucose molecules in Figure A on another sheet of paper. Be sure to draw the dotted lines. Use scissors to cut out the three models of glucose. Cut along the solid lines. Do not cut the dotted lines yet.

3. Form a disaccharide by joining two of the glucose models. To do this, cut the H piece off the right side of Glucose Molecule 1 along the dotted lines. Cut the OH piece off the left side of Glucose Molecule 2 along the dotted lines.

4. Keep the OH and H pieces you cut off. You will use them later in the lab. Put Glucose Molecule 1 and Glucose Molecule 2 together side by side. Connect them at the ends that are missing the H and OH. Glucose Molecule 1 will be on the left. Tape the two molecules together. The union of two glucose molecules produces a maltose molecule.

5. To form a starch molecule, add Glucose Molecule 3 to the maltose molecule. Remove the H from the right side of the maltose molecule (Glucose Molecule 2). Remove the OH from the left side of Glucose Molecule 3. Keep the OH and H pieces. Tape Glucose Molecule 3 to the maltose molecule to form the starch molecule.

6. Tape the starch molecule to your notebook paper. Write a "+" sign after the molecule. Now combine the OH and H groups to form water molecules. Tape these molecules together and attach them to your paper after the "+" sign.

Cleanup/Disposal

Follow your teacher's instructions for cleanup and disposal of materials.

Studying Dehydration Synthesis, continued

Analysis

1. How many molecules of water were removed from the glucose molecules to make maltose?

_____

2. In this lab you made a short molecule of starch. How many water molecules did you have to remove to make the starch molecule?

_____

_____

Conclusions

1. The term *dehydrate* means to remove water. Explain why the creation of starch from glucose molecules is described as a dehydration reaction.

_____

_____

2. If you had more models of glucose, could you add them to your existing starch molecule? If so, how would you do it?

_____

_____

3. If you wanted to take apart your model of starch and make individual models of glucose molecules, what would you do?

_____

_____

_____

Explore Further

Starch and cellulose are both made of long chains of glucose molecules. Find out why the two molecules are different. Describe their differences.

_____

_____

_____

Dehydration Synthesis, continued

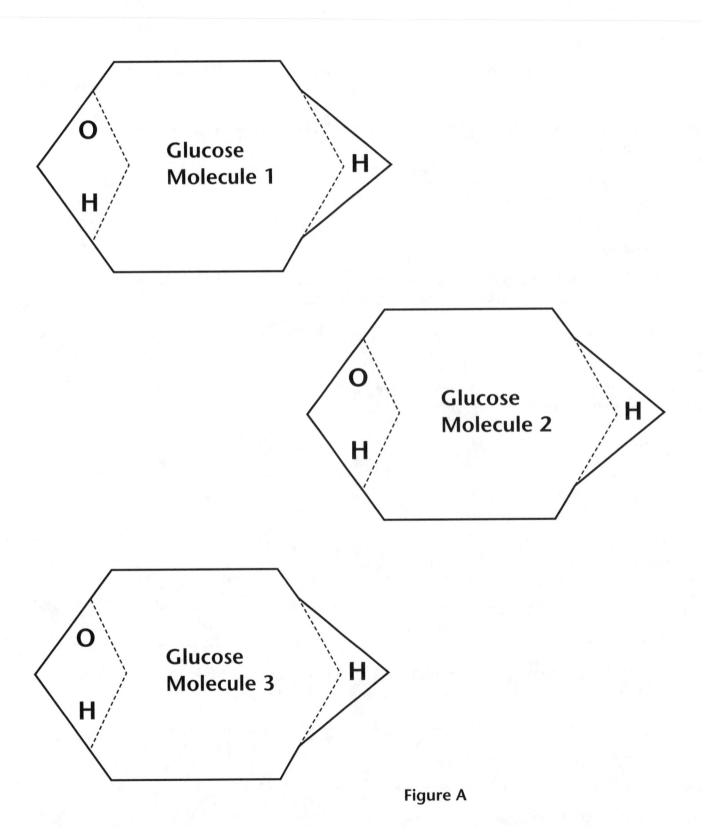

Figure A

Express Lab 3

Use with Express Lab 3, page 74

Materials   Food labels with Nutrition Facts

Procedure

1. Select one food label.

2. Read the label. Determine the amount of fat, carbohydrates, and protein in one serving of the food.

3. Compare your food label with a different food label chosen by a classmate. Which food is higher in fat, carbohydrates, and protein?

Analysis

1. What kinds of carbohydrates are listed on the label?

_____

_____

2. Calculate the percentage of calories from fat in one serving.

_____

_____

Amino Acids and Proteins

Use with Investigation 3, pages 75–76

Proteins are made of monomers called amino acids. How can you tell if a food contains proteins? In this investigation, you will test for proteins.

Materials   safety goggles   test tube rack   5% milk solution
                  lab coat or apron   graduated cylinder   5% starch solution
                  wax pencil   distilled water   dropper bottle of biuret solution
                  test tubes   egg albumin solution

Procedure

1. To record your data, make a data table like the one shown here.

Solution	Color	Protein
1. distilled water		
2. egg albumin solution		
3. 5% milk solution		
4. 5% starch solution		

2. Put on safety goggles and a lab coat or apron. **Safety Alert: Do not touch or taste any chemicals.**

3. With a wax pencil, label four test tubes from 1 to 4. Add 3 mL of each solution to the correct tube: **Test Tube 1** distilled water
                                                                                                              Test Tube 2 egg albumin solution
                                                                                                              Test Tube 3 5% milk solution
                                                                                                              Test Tube 4 5% starch solution

4. Add a dropperful of biuret solution to each tube. Mix gently. Look at the color of each tube. A protein will cause a color change.

5. In your data table, write down your observations.

Cleanup/Disposal

Before leaving the lab, clean up your materials and wash your hands.

Amino Acids and Proteins, continued

Analysis

1. Which tubes contain a protein?

_____

_____

2. What color change do you see if the tube contains a protein?

_____

3. Which tube is a control? _____ Did any of the results surprise you?
Explain your answer.

_____

_____

_____

Conclusions

1. What do all proteins have in common?

_____

_____

2. Why do you think Test Tube 1 contained distilled water?

_____

_____

3. Write a new question about testing for proteins that you could explore in
another investigation.

_____

_____

Explore Further

Use the same procedure to test for proteins in other foods.

Testing for Starches

Plants produce glucose to use as an energy source. If a plant makes more glucose than it needs, the extra molecules are stored in the form of starch. Starch is a carbohydrate made up of long chains of glucose molecules.

Many kinds of animals, including humans, consume the starches in plants. Some of the most popular starch plant products are potatoes, corn, and grains. Grains include wheat and rice. These starches are used to produce a wide variety of foods. In the animal diet, starches serve as quick sources of energy.

In this lab, you will test several kinds of food for the presence of starch. Iodine, a reddish-brown liquid, turns blue or black on starch.

Materials safety goggles
lab coat or apron
10 or more small samples of food (such as cheese, bread,
  raw potato, cooked pasta, luncheon meat, mayonnaise,
  lettuce, tomato, apple, onion, radish, cucumber, milk)
pipette
small bottle of iodine
paper towel

Procedure

1. Put on safety goggles and a lab coat or apron. **Safety Alert: Iodine can permanently stain clothing.**

2. Select 10 food samples and place them on a paper towel.

3. In the left column of the data table at right, list the foods you have selected.

4. Put a drop of iodine on the first sample. If the iodine on the food sample turns blue or black, write "Yes" in the table beside that sample. If the iodine remains the same color, write "No."

5. Follow the same procedure for each food sample.

Food Sample	Turns Iodine Blue/Black
1.	
2.	
3.	
4.	
5.	
6.	
7.	
8.	
9.	
10.	

Testing for Starches, continued

Cleanup/Disposal

Follow your teacher's instructions for cleanup and disposal of materials.

Analysis

1. Of the foods that tested positive for starch, how many of them were of animal origin?

   For example, how many were items such as meat, milk, cheese? _____

   How many were of plant origin, such as bread, potato, onion? _____

2. Circle the three foods that are your personal favorites
   of the ones tested. Are they carbohydrates? _____

Conclusions

1. The black substance produced by the combination of iodine with starch is a
   new substance that did not exist before. Knowing this, is the production of the
   black substance a chemical or physical change? Why?

   _____

   _____

2. Before an important event, an athlete might eat a lot of carbohydrates to stock up on
   energy reserves. Suggest a meal that is rich in carbohydrates.

   _____

   _____

3. Which group of people do you think needs more carbohydrates in their diets:
   people who work at a computer all day or people who load packages on trucks?
   Explain your answer.

   _____

   _____

Explore Further

Starch and cellulose are both made of long chains of glucose molecules. Find out
how the chemical structures of the two macromolecules differ. Explain how the
chemical structures are different.

_____

_____

Testing for Lipids

Use with Discovery Investigation 3, pages 86–87

Lipids contain carbon, hydrogen, and oxygen atoms, but not in the same ratio as carbohydrates. If you were given an unknown substance, how could you tell if it is a lipid? You will find out in this lab.

Materials	safety goggles	water
	lab coat or apron	vegetable oil
	wax pencil	unknown liquid
	test tubes	Sudan III dye solution
	test tube rack	methylene blue dye solution

Procedure

1. To record your data, make a data table like the one shown here.

Solution	Sudan III	Methylene Blue
1. water		
2. vegetable oil		
3. water + oil		

2. Put on safety goggles and a lab coat or apron. **Safety Alert: Do not touch or taste any chemicals.**

3. With a wax pencil, label three test tubes from 1 to 3. Add the following solutions to the correct tube:
Test Tube 1   2 mL water
Test Tube 2   2 mL vegetable oil
Test Tube 3   1 mL water + 1 mL vegetable oil

4. Add 3 drops of Sudan III to each test tube. Then add 3 drops of methylene blue to Test Tube 3. Shake the test tubes well. Allow them to settle.

5. In your data table, write down your observations.

6. In a small group, discuss how you could determine if an unknown liquid is a lipid. Write a hypothesis that could be tested with an experiment using the unknown solution.

Hypothesis: _____

_____

Testing for Lipids, continued

7. Write a procedure for your experiment. Include Safety Alerts.

_____

_____

_____

_____

8. Have your hypothesis, procedure, and Safety Alerts approved by your teacher. Then carry out your experiment. Record your results.

Cleanup/Disposal

Before leaving the lab, clean up your materials and wash your hands.

Analysis

1. What differences did you notice between Test Tube 1 and Test Tube 2?

_____

_____

2. Explain how Sudan III and methylene blue behave differently as dyes.

_____

_____

Conclusions

1. Was your hypothesis supported by the results of your investigation? _____

2. How do the structural differences between lipids and carbohydrates explain your results?

_____

_____

_____

_____

Explore Further

In your group, discuss other ways that you could test an unknown substance to determine if it is a lipid.

Express Lab 4

Use with Express Lab 4, page 107

Materials   safety goggles
                  lab coat or apron
                  eyedropper
                  pond water or hay infusion
                  microscope slide
                  coverslip
                  microscope

Procedure

1. Put on safety goggles and a lab coat or apron.

2. Use the eyedropper to get a drop of pond water or hay infusion.

3. Place the drop on a microscope slide. Hold a coverslip at a 45° angle from the slide and at the edge of the drop of solution. Gently lower the coverslip over the drop. **Safety Alert: Handle glass microscope slides with care. Dispose of broken glass properly.**

4. Use a microscope to examine the slide under low power and then under high power. Describe the different kinds of cells you see.

5. When finished, wash your hands well.

Analysis

1. How many kinds of cells did you find?

_____

_____

2. Were any cells moving? If so, describe them.

_____

_____

_____

_____

Cork Cells

In 1665, Robert Hooke examined a very thin slice of cork under his microscope. Hooke noticed that cork is made up of air surrounded by grids of supporting structures. Because the air chambers reminded him of the small rooms or cells in monasteries, he named them cells. The name stuck and is still used today. What Hooke saw was the cell walls of cork, a plant. At that time, he did not realize that cells are the most basic units of living things. In this lab, you will recreate Hooke's experiment.

Materials

safety goggles   small piece of cork
lab coat or apron   eyedropper
microscope   water
microscope slide   pen or pencil
coverslip   paper
razor or scalpel

Procedure

1. Put on safety goggles and a lab coat or apron.

2. Use the razor blade to carefully trim off a very thin piece of cork. The thinner your sample, the better. **Safety Alert: Take special care when working with the razor blade or scalpel.**

3. Remove goggles and set aside.

4. Place the thin slice of cork on a microscope slide.

5. Use the eyedropper to add a drop of water to the slide.

6. Hold a coverslip at a 45° angle at the edge of the water drop. Gently lower the coverslip over the water and cork.

7. Place the slide on the microscope stage. Follow your teacher's instructions for focusing the microscope.

8. Make a sketch of what you see on low, medium, and high power.

9. On the high power drawing, label two individual cells.

10. Count the number of cork cells that are visible on high power.

Cork Cells, continued

Cleanup and Disposal

Follow your teacher's instructions for cleanup and disposal of materials.

Analysis

1. How many cork cells did you see under high power?

_____

2. Describe any structures that you can see under high power.

_____

Conclusions

1. Cork is part of a plant. In plants, each living cell is surrounded by a thin, transparent membrane and a sturdy cell wall. What parts of the plant cell did you see under high power?

_____

2. Based on your observations, do you think that cork cells are dead or alive? Explain your answer.

_____

_____

3. If you were the first person to see a sample of cork under the microscope, what would you name the individual units?

_____

_____

Explore Further

Compare cork cells to the cells of bamboo. Write a short paragraph about their similarities and differences.

_____

_____

_____

_____

Living Cells

Use with Investigation 4, pages 109–110

The cell is the basic unit of life. Yeasts are single-celled organisms. In this lab, you will see how yeast cells perform the functions necessary for life.

Materials

safety goggles	1 envelope active dry yeast
lab coat or apron	eyedropper
100 mL beaker	microscope slide
sucrose	dropper bottle of iodine solution
warm water (38°C to 43°C)	coverslip
glass rod	microscope

Procedure

1. Put on safety goggles and a lab coat or apron.

2. In a 100 mL beaker, add 4 g sucrose to 60 mL warm water. With a glass rod, stir in one envelope of active dry yeast. Let the mixture stand for 10 minutes.

3. Describe the appearance of the mixture in the beaker.

_____

_____

4. Use the eyedropper to place one drop of the mixture onto a clean glass microscope slide. **Safety Alert: Handle glass microscope slides with care. Dispose of broken glass properly.**

5. Add one drop of iodine solution to the mixture on the slide. **Safety Alert: Iodine stains skin and clothing. It is a poison and an eye irritant.**

6. Hold a coverslip at a 45° angle at the edge of the drop of iodine solution. Gently lower the coverslip over the drop. You have prepared a wet mount.

7. Place the wet mount on the microscope stage. Follow instructions from your teacher to focus and adjust the microscope.

8. Observe several yeast cells. Make note of their shape.

_____

_____

Living Cells, continued

Cleanup/Disposal

Before leaving the lab, clean up your materials and wash your hands.

Analysis

1. What is the energy source for yeast cells?

_____

_____

2. What cell structure surrounds each yeast cell?

_____

_____

Conclusions

1. What is the role of the cell membrane?

_____

_____

_____

2. Write a new question about energy and living cells that you could explore in another investigation.

_____

_____

Explore Further

Design a similar procedure to test the effects of temperature on living yeast cells.

_____

_____

_____

_____

Diffusion

The cell is separated from the environment by a membrane. Molecules move into and out of the cell by diffusing through the membrane. Diffusion is the movement of molecules from an area of high concentration to an area of lower concentration. For example, every cell gets its supply of oxygen from the blood. Oxygen dissolved in blood diffuses into cells. Carbon dioxide gas, a waste product, diffuses from the cells into the blood. The process of diffusion moves many life-sustaining molecules through cell membranes.

Materials   safety goggles
               lab coat or apron
               200 mL beaker
               dropper bottle of ink or blue dye
               water
               pen or pencil
               paper
               watch or clock with a second hand

Procedure

1. Put on safety goggles and a lab coat or apron.

2. Fill the 200 mL beaker with water.

3. On your paper, draw four identical pictures of beakers holding 200 mL of water.

4. Label the picture of the first beaker as 0 minutes. Label the picture of the second beaker as 5 minutes. Label the third beaker as 10 minutes and the fourth beaker as 15 minutes.

5. Place one drop of ink or blue dye in the beaker of water. Draw the appearance of the dye in water in the picture labeled 0 minutes.

6. Draw the appearance of the dye in the beaker of water after 5 minutes, 10 minutes, and 15 minutes. In each drawing, show how the shape and size of the ink or blue dye has changed.

Diffusion, continued

Cleanup and Disposal

Follow your teacher's instructions for cleanup and disposal of materials.

Analysis

1. At the beginning of the experiment, where was the ink or blue dye most concentrated in the beaker?

_____

2. Describe what happened to the ink or blue dye during the 15 minutes that you observed the beaker.

_____

_____

_____

Conclusions

1. What process caused the ink or blue dye to change positions in the beaker?

_____

2. If you had let the beaker of ink or blue dye and water sit overnight, what would you expect to see on the second day?

_____

_____

3. Why does a teabag in a cup of water change the color of the water?

_____

_____

Explore Further

Compare the rate of diffusion of ink or blue dye in ice water and in warm water. Record your results.

Osmosis in Cells

Use with Discovery Investigation 4, pages 121–122

Water enters and leaves cells by osmosis. In this investigation, you will predict the direction of water movement across a cell membrane. Under what conditions will water enter a cell? Under what conditions will water leave a cell?

Materials

safety goggles
lab coat or apron
microscope slide
forceps
Elodea leaf

dropper bottle of distilled water
coverslip
microscope
dropper bottle of 10% NaCl solution

Procedure

1. Put on safety goggles and a lab coat or apron.

2. Use forceps to get a small *Elodea* leaf. Use the dropper to put a drop of distilled water onto a clean glass microscope slide. Place the leaf on the drop of water. Carefully place a coverslip on the drop. **Safety Alert: Handle glass microscope slides with care. Dispose of broken glass properly.**

3. Place the wet mount on the microscope stage. Follow instructions from your teacher to focus and adjust the microscope.

4. Describe what you see. Do you think water is entering the *Elodea* cells or leaving the cells? Explain your answer.

_____

_____

_____

_____

_____

5. In a small group, discuss how you could determine the conditions that cause water to enter and exit the cell. Write a hypothesis that you could test with an experiment.

Hypothesis: _____

_____

Osmosis in Cells, continued

6. Write a procedure for your experiment. Include Safety Alerts.

_____

_____

_____

_____

7. Have your hypothesis, procedure, and Safety Alerts approved by your teacher. Then carry out your experiment. Record your results.

Cleanup/Disposal

Before leaving the lab, clean up your materials and wash your hands.

Analysis

1. Is distilled water a hypotonic or hypertonic environment for _Elodea_ cells?

_____

2. In what direction do you think water would move if _Elodea_ cells were surrounded by saltwater?

_____

_____

Conclusions

1. Was your hypothesis supported by the results of your investigation?

_____

2. Plant fertilizers contain salts. Why is it important to use the correct amount of fertilizer?

_____

_____

_____

Explore Further

In your group, discuss how you could find out if the events you have just seen are reversible.

Express Lab 5

Use with Express Lab 5, page 135

What elements are in common household products? In this investigation, you will examine the chemical makeup of common products in the home.

Materials   safety goggles
lab coat or apron
medium-sized beaker
warm tap water
vegetable oil

Procedure

1. Put on safety goggles and a lab coat or apron.

2. Fill the beaker about one-quarter full of water.
   Safety Alert: Be careful when working with glassware.

3. Add vegetable oil until the beaker is about half full of liquid.

4. Observe the liquids in the beaker. Gently tilt the beaker back and forth. Observe how the liquids respond to the motion.

Analysis

1. Which liquid is like the head of a phospholipid? _____

   Which liquid is like the tail? _____

2. How did the liquids respond when you tilted the beaker sideways?

   _____

   _____

   How is this similar to a plasma membrane?

   _____

   _____

A Day in the Life of a Protein

Every living thing is made up of cells. Each cell is so small that it can only be seen under the microscope. The human body contains trillions of these tiny cells.

Not all of the cells in the body are alike or have the same job. Skin cells cover the surface and the body and protect it. Muscle cells make it possible to move. Cells of the skeleton support the body structure. Nerve cells carry electrical impulses.

Despite their differences, all kinds of cells have a lot in common. In this lab, you will make a working model of a few of the structures found in all cells. You will use the model to simulate some of the events that might occur in a day in the life of a protein.

Materials   construction paper
markers or crayons
scissors
modeling clay (about the size of a golf ball)
10–12 thumbtacks

Procedure

1. The following table indicates the lab materials that represent cell parts.

Lab Material	Cell Part
construction paper models	nucleus, rough endoplasmic reticulum, Golgi apparatus, vacuole, lysosome
clay	protein
thumbtacks	molecules added to proteins
desktop	cytoplasm
edge of desktop	plasma membrane

2. On construction paper, draw a cell nucleus, rough endoplasmic reticulum, Golgi apparatus, vacuole, and lysosome. Use Figure B on page 3 of this lab as a model. Make your drawings much bigger than those in the model. For example, the nucleus could be as large as your hand.

3. Cut out your drawings. **Safety Alert: Be careful when using scissors.**
Arrange them on your desktop similar to the way they are arranged in Figure B on page 3.

A Day in the Life of a Protein, continued

4. Spread the thumbtacks through the Golgi apparatus. **Safety Alert: Handle thumbtacks with care. They are sharp.**

5. Ribosomes make proteins. One of the places where ribosomes can be found is on the rough endoplasmic reticulum (RER). Break off a piece of modeling clay about the size of a quarter. Place it in the RER. The clay represents a protein made in the RER.

6. Vacuoles move proteins and other materials around the cell. Move the protein from the RER into the vacuole. Push the vacuole with its protein to one end of the Golgi apparatus.

7. In the Golgi apparatus, proteins are modified slightly. Transfer the protein to the Golgi apparatus. Roll the protein slowly through the Golgi apparatus, adding 2 or 3 thumbtacks to it. The thumbtacks represent molecules that prepare the protein for a specific job.

8. Once a protein is modified, it is released into the cell to do its work. Transfer the modified protein to the vacuole. Move the modified protein to a location of your choice in the cell. Remove the protein from the vacuole.

9. Repeat steps 5 through 8 two more times so that you have a group of three modified proteins.

10. After doing its work, a protein is broken down and its parts are recycled. Lysosomes break down proteins and other materials in cells. Place one modified protein into the lysosome. Pull the thumbtacks out of the clay and return them to the Golgi apparatus. Flatten the clay ball and move it into the cytoplasm.

11. Repeat step 10 with the other two modified proteins.

Cleanup/Disposal

Follow your teacher's instructions for cleanup and disposal of materials.

Analysis

1. What is the job of the vacuole?

_____

_____

2. What is the job of the lysosome?

_____

_____

A Day in the Life of a Protein, continued

Conclusions

1. Cells export some proteins. What might happen in a day of a protein destined for export?

_____

_____

2. What are some possible reasons for modifying proteins?

_____

_____

3. Do you think that the activities of proteins require energy? Explain your answer.

_____

_____

Explore Further

The cell in this lab is an animal cell. Create a model of a plant cell. Compare the activities of proteins in each type of cell.

_____

_____

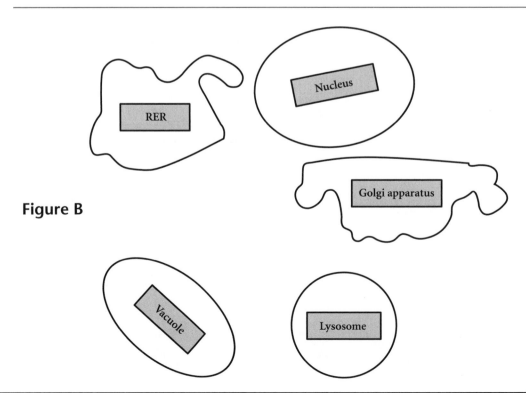

Figure B

Cells Made of Gelatin

In textbooks, pictures of cells are flat and two-dimensional. In a living thing, cells are actually three-dimensional structures. The organelles in cells are not spread out in a thin, evenly distributed layer as they appear in a picture. Some organelles may be on the top of the cell, while others are on the bottom. The nucleus may not be located in the center of a cell, and can be found in any location. In this lab, you will see how the parts of the cell that can be seen under the microscope depend on where the cell was sectioned.

Materials   safety goggles   spoon
                  lab coat or apron   knife
                  1 self-sealing plastic bag (pint size) $1\frac{1}{2}$ cups water
                  1 envelope of unflavored gelatin   hot plate
                  small saucepan   variety of small fruits or vegetables,
                  hot pads   dried peas and beans, and uncooked noodles
                  measuring cup   (to represent organelles)

Procedure

1. Put on safety goggles and a lab coat or apron.

2. Place $1\frac{1}{2}$ cups of water in the saucepan. Put the saucepan on the hot plate. Heat water until boiling. **Safety Alerts: Take care when working with hot water and the hot plate. Be careful when using the knife.**

3. Pour 1 envelope of unflavored gelatin in the measuring cup. Add boiling water to make one cup. Stir to completely dissolve gelatin.

4. Pour gelatin into the plastic bag. Let the bag of gelatin cool to room temperature.

5. Place peas, beans, pasta, or fruit into the bag. These items represent organelles. For example, small peas could represent ribosomes, orange slices mitochondria, and long noodles endoplasmic reticulum. Include other items to represent the nucleus, Golgi apparatus, lysosome, and vacuole.

6. Seal the plastic bag and refrigerate overnight.

7. On day 2, observe the bag and its contents.

8. Peel the plastic bag off the gelatin cell.

9. With a knife, make a cross section of the cell. Examine the organelles that are visible on the cut surfaces.

Cells Made of Gelatin, continued

Cleanup/Disposal

Follow your teacher's instructions for cleanup and disposal of materials.

Analysis

1. In this experiment, what represents the cell membrane? _____

What represents the cytoplasm? _____

2. What structures were visible when you cut your gelatin cell in half?

_____

Would these same structures have been visible if you had sliced the cell

in a different place? Explain your answer.

_____

_____

3. Is this a plant or animal cell? _____

How do you know? _____

_____

Conclusions

1. How could the entire class work together to create a sample of "gelatin tissue"?

_____

_____

2. If you were a scientist studying the parts of cells, would you learn more
by observing living cells or by slicing and observing dead cells? Explain your answer.

_____

_____

Explore Further

Create a plant cell of gelatin. Use a dish or pan to represent the cell wall.

Comparing Plant and Animal Cells

Use with Investigation 5, pages 157–158

All organisms are made up of cells. All cells have some things in common. However, some key differences exist between the cells that make up plants and the cells that make up animals. In this lab, you will examine plant cells and animal cells, noting their similarities and differences.

Materials
safety goggles	dropper bottle of iodine solution
lab coat or apron	coverslip
tweezers	microscope
onion	prepared slide of human cheek cells
glass slide	

Procedure

1. Put on safety goggles and a lab coat or apron.

2. Using tweezers, peel a small, thin piece of tissue from an inside section of the onion.

3. Place the piece of onion tissue on a glass slide. Be sure the piece of onion is small enough to fit on the slide. **Safety Alert: Handle glass microscope slides with care. Dispose of broken glass properly.**

4. Add one drop of iodine solution to the onion piece on the slide. **Safety Alert: Iodine stains skin and clothing. It is a poison and an eye irritant.**

5. Hold a coverslip at a 45° angle at the edge of the drop of iodine solution. Gently lower the coverslip.

6. Look at the onion cells under the microscope. Observe the cells at various magnifications until you get a clear, sharp image.

7. Make a drawing of what you see under the microscope. Label your drawing.

8. Next, look at the prepared slide of human cheek cells under the microscope. Make a drawing of what you see. Label your drawing.

Cleanup/Disposal

Before leaving the lab, clean up your materials and wash your hands.

Comparing Plant and Animal Cells, continued

Analysis

1. Which cell parts were you able to identify in the onion and cheek cells?

_____

_____

2. What differences did you observe between the two types of cells?

_____

_____

Conclusions

1. What organelles were you not able to find as you observed the cells?

_____

_____

Why do you think you could not find them?

_____

_____

2. How do the differences in the two types of cells reflect the differences
in the organisms the cells belong to?

_____

_____

_____

Explore Further

Observe cells from other sections of the onion. How do they compare with
the first cells you observed?

_____

_____

_____

_____

Comparing Plant Cells

Use with Discovery Investigation 5, pages 161–162

The cells in different parts of a plant are different depending on the jobs of those particular cells. In this lab, you will examine cells from different parts of a plant. You will discover how the parts differ according to their functions.

Materials   *Elodea* plant   glass slide
safety goggles   coverslip
lab coat or apron   microscope
tweezers   prepared slide of onion root tip
eyedropper   (longitudinal section)
distilled water   prepared slide of corn stem (cross section)

Procedure

1. Put on safety goggles and a lab coat or apron.

2. In a small group, observe an *Elodea* plant. Discuss the structure of its leaves, stems, and roots. Make a table that lists the characteristics of each plant part.

3. Predict what differences you will find in the cells of the three plant parts.

4. Make a wet mount of one *Elodea* leaf using a drop of water.

5. Examine the wet mount under a microscope. Observe the cells at various magnifications until you get a clear, sharp image. Discuss what you see. Record your observations. Make a drawing of the cells you observe. Label the cell parts in your drawing. **Safety Alert: Handle glass microscope slides with care. Dispose of broken glass properly.**

6. Observe the cells in the prepared slide of a corn stem. Discuss and record your observations. Make and label a drawing of the cells.

7. Observe the cells in the prepared slide of an onion root tip. Discuss and record your observations. Make and label a drawing of the cells.

Cleanup/Disposal

Before leaving the lab, clean up your materials and wash your hands.

Comparing Plant Cells, continued

Analysis

1. What plant organelles did you see?

_____

_____

2. What differences did you notice in the cells and arrangements of cells
in the three plant parts?

_____

_____

Conclusions

1. How accurate were your predictions compared with what you observed?

_____

2. As a group, select another type of plant. Predict what you might find in
different parts of the plant you have selected.

_____

_____

_____

Explore Further

Research one of the following plant structures: potato, thorn, celery stalk, lettuce,

or onion bulb. Is the structure a root, stem, or leaf? _____

What makes this structure different from a typical root, stem, or leaf?

_____

_____

What would you expect to find if you examined its cells?

_____

_____

Express Lab 6

Use with Express Lab 6, page 172

Materials   3 tennis balls
meterstick

Procedure

1. Set one tennis ball on the ground. Set a second tennis ball on a desk or a table. Set a third tennis ball on a shelf or a place that is higher than the desk or table.

2. Push the tennis ball off the desk or table. With a meterstick, measure how high the tennis ball bounces. Record this measurement.

3. Push the tennis ball off the shelf or from the high place. With a meterstick, measure how high the tennis ball bounces. Record this measurement.

Analysis

1. Which tennis ball had the most potential energy?

_____

2. Which tennis ball had the least potential energy?

_____

3. How did you transfer the potential energy of the tennis balls to kinetic energy?

_____

_____

4. What do the bounce height measurements tell you about the kinetic and potential energy of the three tennis balls?

_____

_____

The Structure of ATP

A cell is powered by chemical energy that is stored in molecules of ATP, adenosine triphosphate. When a molecule of ATP releases energy, it loses a phosphate group and changes into ADP, adenosine diphosphate. ADP can change back into ATP with the input of energy and the addition of a phosphate group.

Every ATP molecule has three basic parts: a ribose molecule, an adenine molecule, and three phosphate molecules. An ADP molecule is very similar, but has only two phosphate molecules. The breakdown and formation of ADP and ATP is cyclic. In this lab, you will make models of ADP and ATP molecules.

Materials   patterns in Figure C

scissors

tape

Procedure

1. Trace the shapes in Figure C on page 2 on a sheet of paper. Then cut out the shapes you traced by cutting along the solid lines. **Safety Alert: Take care when working with scissors.**

2. Examine the adenine and ribose molecules to see if you can fit them together like puzzle pieces. Notice that they will not fit together until you cut away an OH group on ribose and an H on adenine. With your scissors, make these cuts along the dotted lines. (Do not throw away the cut pieces.)

3. Fit adenine and ribose together. Tape the two molecules in place. Fit the leftover pieces of OH and H together.

4. Examine the ribose and one of the phosphate groups. To fit these two pieces together, cut along the dotted lines to remove the H from the phosphate group and the OH from the ribose. Tape the two molecules together. Fit the leftover pieces of OH and H together and tape into place.

5. Join another phosphate group to the one already taped to your model. Remove the appropriate H and OH groups first. Then tape the phosphate in place and tape together the leftover OH and H.

6. Trim the last phosphate group and the phosphate end of your model so that one more phosphate can be added. Do not tape this last phosphate in place at this time. Lay it in the appropriate position on your model. Tape together the leftover OH and H.

The Structure of ATP, continued

Cleanup/Disposal

Follow your teacher's instructions for cleanup and disposal of materials.

Analysis

1. When all three phosphate groups are lined up with adenine and ribose,

what molecule does your model represent? _____

2. When you remove the unattached phosphate group from your model,

what molecule does your model represent? _____

3. What do the prefixes *di-* and *tri-* stand for?

_____

Conclusions

1. Describe the chemical reaction in which a molecule of ATP is formed.

_____

_____

2. What role does hydrolysis play in the formation of ADP?

_____

Explore Further

Using your model to help you visualize the reactants and products, write a
chemical equation for the hydrolysis of ATP.

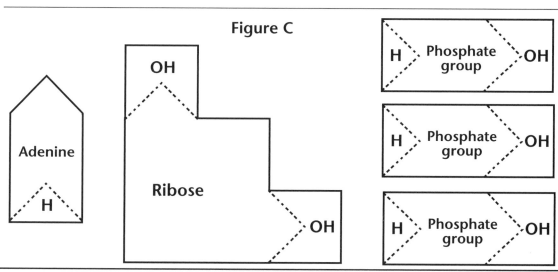

Figure C

Enzymes in Saliva

Use with Investigation 6, pages 178–179

Your body uses enzymes to help digest food. When you eat, enzymes in your saliva help breakdown the sugars in food for your cells to use. In this lab, you will observe how the enzyme amylase found in saliva breaks down starches. You will test reactions with Benedict's reagent and iodine solution. Benedict's reagent changes color from blue to yellow if sugar, such as maltose, is present. Iodine turns blue or black in the presence of starch.

Materials

safety goggles	maltose solution	warm water
lab coat or apron	starch solution	eyedropper
wax pencil	1% amylase solution	iodine solution
6 test tubes	250 mL beaker	Benedict's reagent
test tube rack		

Procedure

1. To record your data, make a data table like the one shown here.

Test Tube	Contents	Iodine Test	Benedict's Test
1	maltose (sugar)		
2	starch + amylase		
3	starch + maltose (sugar)		

2. Put on safety goggles and a lab coat or apron.

3. With a wax pencil, label three test tubes 1, 2, and 3. Label a second set of three test tubes in the same way and set them aside.

4. Add 2 mL of maltose solution to Test Tube 1.

5. Add 2 mL of starch solution to Test Tubes 2 and 3.

6. Add 4 mL of water to Test Tubes 1 and 3.

7. Add 4 mL of amylase solution to Test Tube 2.

8. To make a warm water bath, fill a 250 mL beaker with 150 mL of warm water.

9. Place all three test tubes in the warm water bath for 15 minutes. Be sure the test tubes stand upright. Do not allow water to enter the test tubes.

10. Remove the test tubes from the water batch. Pour half of the contents of each test tube into the empty test tubes with the same label.

Enzymes in Saliva, continued

11. For each pair, use the wax pencil to label one test tube I for iodine test and the other B for Benedict's test.

12. Place two drops of iodine solution in one of the Test Tube 1-I. Gently swirl the test tube. Record your observations in the data table. Place two drops of Benedict's reagent in Test Tube 1-B. Gently swirl the tube. Record your observations.

13. Repeat Step 12 for Test Tubes 2-I and 2-B, and 3-I and 3-B.

Cleanup/Disposal

Before leaving the lab, follow your teacher's instructions to clean up and dispose of your materials.

Analysis

1. What happened to the starch when amylase was added to it?

_____

_____

2. Which solutions tested positive for sugar? _____

Which solutions tested positive for starch? _____

Conclusions

1. Why did you use maltose in one of your test tubes? _____

_____

2. How does amylase work in your body? _____

_____

Where in your body do these processes take place? _____

3. Why is it important for you to chew your food well when you eat?

_____

_____

Explore Further

Try the test again using a starchy food such as corn, rice, or potatoes. Be sure you chop up the food before putting it in the test tube. This chopping represents the action of chewing before digestion.

The Action of an Enzyme

Enzymes are proteins that change the rates of chemical reactions in living things. Without enzymes, chemical reactions would occur too slowly to support life. Every cell contains hundreds of different enzymes, all performing essential jobs. During chemical reactions, enzymes are not changed.

Because enzymes are proteins, they are sensitive to temperature. The body maintains enzymes at a constant temperature. Heat and cold can interfere with their abilities to cause chemical reactions.

Living tissues contain the enzyme peroxidase. Liver tissue is especially rich in this particular enzyme. The job of peroxidase is to break down hydrogen peroxide into harmless oxygen gas and water. Hydrogen peroxide is a natural by-product of cellular respiration. If hydrogen peroxide builds up in tissue, it can cause damage.

Materials   safety goggles   test tube rack   hot pads
             lab coat or apron   scalpel or knife   hot water (200 mL beaker of
             piece of liver (about the   tape or labels   water warmed on a hot plate)
               size of a quarter)   hydrogen peroxide $\frac{1}{2}$ cup of crushed ice
             3 test tubes   forceps   polystyrene cup
                                                                    timer or clock

Procedure

1. Put on safety goggles and a lab coat or apron.

2. Label the test tubes as A, B, and C. Place Test Tubes A and B in the test tube rack. Place Test Tube C in the cup of ice.

3. Cut the quarter-size piece of liver into 3 smaller pieces of about equal size.
   Safety Alert: Take care when working with the scalpel.

4. Place one piece of liver in Test Tube C.

5. With forceps, place a second piece of liver in the hot water and let it cook for 2 minutes.

6. After two minutes, use the forceps to remove the liver from the hot water. Put the liver in Test Tube B.

7. Place the third piece of liver in Test Tube A. This represents the control.

8. Fill Test Tube A one-quarter full with hydrogen peroxide. Notice how many bubbles are produced as peroxidase in the liver breaks the hydrogen peroxide into water and oxygen. On a scale of 0 to 5, with 5 as extremely bubbly and 0 as not bubbling, rate the level of bubble activity. Record this rating in the data table.

The Action of an Enzyme, continued

9. Fill Test Tube B one-quarter full with hydrogen peroxide. Notice how many bubbles are produced and rate the bubble activity from 0 to 5. Record this rating in the data table.

10. Fill Test Tube C one-quarter full with hydrogen peroxide. Notice how many bubbles are produced. Rate the bubble activity from 0 to 5. Record this rating in the data table.

Test Tube	Bubble Activity Rating
A	
B	
C	

Cleanup/Disposal

Follow your teacher's instructions for cleanup and disposal of materials.

Analysis

1. Which liver sample produced the most bubbles: A, B, or C? _____

2. How did boiling affect bubbling?

_____

How did cooling affect bubbling?

_____

Conclusions

1. Enzymes are found in the human body. At what temperature do you

think enzymes function best? _____

2. Bubbling is a reflection of enzyme activity. How was the function of the enzyme

peroxidase changed by heat? _____

_____

How was it changed by cold? _____

_____

The Action of an Enzyme, continued

3. Peroxidase is in human blood. Explain why hydrogen peroxide applied to a cut causes bubbling.

_____

_____

Explore Further

Compare the activity of the enzyme peroxidase to the activity of a catalyst. Manganese dioxide is a catalyst that speeds the breakdown of hydrogen peroxide.

_____

_____

_____

How Does pH Affect Stomach Enzymes?

Use with Discovery Investigation 6, pages 187–188

Pepsin is an enzyme that digests proteins. The stomach releases pepsin to break down proteins into peptides and amino acids for digestion. The stomach's environment is full of dilute hydrochloric acid, or HCl. HCl is a strong, irritating acid. Pepsin works well in an acidic environment. In this lab, you will create a procedure to test the activity of pepsin over time at different pH levels. You will use pieces of boiled egg as the protein substrate. You will test samples at different times to see how quickly the egg is digested at different pH levels.

Materials
safety goggles	cool tap water	pieces of boiled egg whites
lab coat or apron	diluted sodium hydroxide	eyedropper
6 test tubes	diluted hydrochloric acid	large beaker
test tube rack	wax pencil	warm water
2% pepsin solution		

Procedure

1. Put on safety goggles and a lab coat or apron.

2. Fill five test tubes half full of the 2% pepsin solution. Be sure each test tube contains the same amount of solution. Create a control by filling a sixth test tube half full of cool tap water. Using the wax pencil, label the control C.

3. Determine the pH levels you want to use in your experiment.

4. You should text a minimum of three pH levels (acidic, neutral, and basic), but you can test up to five. With a wax pencil, number the test tubes. On a sheet of paper, write each pH level and assign it a test tube number. This is your data table. Have your teacher approve your pH levels and data table.

5. Using the eyedropper, add sodium hydroxide to the basic test tube(s) and hydrochloric acid to the acidic test tube(s). Add different amounts according to the variety of pH levels you want. For the neutral pH and control test tubes, do not add either. **Safety Alert: Be careful with diluted hydrochloric acid. Although diluted, it can damage skin, eyes, and clothing. If it spills, rinse the area immediately.**

6. Add a piece of boiled egg white to every test tube. Be sure the pieces are all the same size.

7. Fill the beaker half full with warm water. The water level should be below the top of the test tubes. Place the test tubes in this warm water bath. Be sure the test tubes stand upright with their openings clear of the surface. Water should not enter the test tubes.

How Does pH Affect Stomach Enzymes?, continued

8. Observe how the pepsin breaks down the egg whites at each pH level. Record your observations in your table. At regular time intervals, estimate how much of the egg white is broken down in each test tube. Use your control for comparison.

Cleanup/Disposal

Ask your teacher for guidance in disposing of the solutions. Before leaving the lab, wash your hands.

Analysis

1. How did pH affect the rate at which the egg white was digested?

_____

2. At what pH level did the pepsin work best?

_____

Conclusions

1. What kind of environment does your stomach need to maintain to digest proteins well?

_____

2. Why did you place the test tubes in a warm water bath?

_____

Explore Further

Why do people take antacids? What effect do you think antacids have on your stomach and digestion?

_____

_____

_____

Express Lab 7

Use with Express Lab 7, page 198

Materials   ingredients list from a food label
dictionary or encyclopedia

Procedure

1. Select a food label.

2. Read the ingredients list on your label. Which items are sugars?
Look up unfamiliar ingredients in the dictionary or encyclopedia.

3. Compare your ingredients list with those of your classmates.

Analysis

1. Which food label has the largest number of different sugars?

_____

2. Which food labels list a carbohydrate as the first, second,
or third ingredient?

_____

Products of Cellular Respiration

Use with Investigation 7, pages 206–207

During cellular respiration, cells use glucose and oxygen to make energy in the form of ATP. Cells also release carbon dioxide (CO_2) and water. When carbon dioxide dissolves in water, it forms carbonic acid (H_2CO_3). In this lab, you will see evidence of cellular respiration.

Materials   safety goggles
lab coat or apron
small beaker
ruler
bromothymol blue
plastic wrap
soda straw

Procedure

1. Put on safety goggles and a lab coat or apron.

2. Using a ruler to measure, pour 1 inch of bromothymol blue into a small beaker. On a sheet of paper, describe the color of the liquid in the beaker.
Safety Alert: Be careful when working with glassware and the solution.

3. Cover the beaker with plastic wrap. With a soda straw, poke a small hole through the plastic. Fit the soda straw through the hole.

4. Gently blow through the straw into the beaker. **Safety Alert: Be careful not to splash or inhale the solution.**

5. On a sheet of paper, write a description of your results.

Cleanup/Disposal

Before leaving the lab, clean up your materials and wash your hands.

Products of Cellular Respiration, continued

Analysis

1. When you blow through the soda straw, what happens to the color of the liquid?

   _____

2. Why does the air you exhale cause these results?

   _____

3. What is the source of the carbon atoms in the CO_2 that is released during cellular respiration?

   _____

Conclusions

1. What product of cellular respiration causes the result you observed?

   _____

2. How do you think exercise affects cellular respiration? Explain your answer.

   _____

   _____

Explore Further

Use the procedure above to test the effects of exercise on cellular respiration.

Cabbage Fermentation

Fermentation is a process that produces energy. Many bacteria use fermentation rather than cellular respiration because it can take place without oxygen. During fermentation, glucose produces ATP and some products. The products vary with the type of bacteria. Bacteria produce products like alcohol, lactic acid, and carbon dioxide.

In this lab, you will ferment cabbage. To do so, you will create conditions in which bacteria can grow in the cabbage. As the cabbage ferments, it changes to sauerkraut.

Materials   safety goggles   100 mL salt (NaCl) solution*
                   lab coat or apron   pH paper
                   test tube   balloon (to fit over test tube)
                   test tube rack   graph paper
                   $\frac{1}{4}$ cup of shredded cabbage

Procedure

1. Put on safety goggles and a lab coat or apron.

2. Fill the test tube with shredded cabbage.

3. Cover the cabbage with salt solution.

4. Use pH paper to test the pH of the salt solution. Record the pH in the data table under "Day 0."

5. Observe the color of the cabbage. Smell the cabbage and salt water solution. Describe the appearance and smell in the data table.

6. Cover the mouth of the test tube with a balloon.

7. After 24 hours, remove the balloon and test the pH of the salt water. Record the pH in the data table under "Day 1." Observe the cabbage and smell the cabbage and salt water solution. Describe the appearance and smell in the data table.

8. Repeat step 7 on the next nine days.

9. Make a graph showing the change in pH from Day 0 through Day 10.

---

* *To make 100 mL of 2.5 percent salt solution, dissolve 2.5 grams of NaCl in 97.5 mL of water and stir.*

Cabbage Fermentation, continued

Day	pH	Description of Appearance and Smell
0		
1		
2		
3		
4		
5		
6		
7		
8		
9		
10		

Analysis

1. How did the pH of the cabbage and salt water change over time?

_____

2. How did the size and shape of the balloon change each day?

_____

Conclusions

1. As bacteria grew in the cabbage, how did the cabbage change?

_____

2. How did bacteria affect the pH of the cabbage and salt water?

_____

3. What are two products of fermentation that you observed in the lab?

_____

Explore Further

Try fermenting other vegetables to see if you get the same kinds of results.

Making ATP Without Oxygen

Use with Discovery Investigation 7, pages 212–213

When oxygen is not present, some species use fermentation to make ATP. What are the products of fermentation? Does temperature affect the rate of fermentation? You will find out the answers to these questions in this lab.

Materials
safety goggles
lab coat or apron
large beaker
warm water (38° to 43°C)
large test tube
solution of yeast and sucrose

one-hole rubber stopper with
  gas delivery tube
small beaker
tap water
limewater

Procedure

1. Put on safety goggles and a lab coat or apron.

2. Fill a large beaker half full with warm water.

3. Fill a large test tube nearly full with the solution of yeast and sucrose. Cap the test tube with the one-hole rubber stopper containing the gas delivery tube.

4. **Safety Alert: Be careful when working with glassware.** Place the test tube in the beaker of warm water. Keep the test tube upright. Do not stir or mix the yeast and sucrose solution in the test tube.

5. Fill a small beaker nearly full with tap water. Put the end of the gas delivery tube in the small beaker of tap water. Watch for gas bubbles at the end of the tube. Count the number of gas bubbles released per minute.

6. In a small group, discuss what gas is given off in this setup. Write a hypothesis about how you might identify this gas. The hypothesis should be one that you could test using limewater.

7. Write a procedure and Safety Alerts for your experiment.

8. Have your hypothesis, Safety Alerts, and procedure approved by your teacher. Then carry out your experiment.

Making ATP Without Oxygen, continued

Cleanup/Disposal

Before leaving the lab, clean up your materials and wash your hands.

Analysis

1. How do yeast cells make ATP?

   _____

   _____

2. Is fermentation occurring during your experiment? Describe the evidence that supports your answer.

   _____

   _____

   _____

Conclusions

1. Was your hypothesis supported by the results of your experiment?

   _____

2. Does temperature affect the rate of fermentation? Suggest an experiment that you could perform to find out.

   _____

   _____

Explore Further

In your group, discuss how you could measure the effect of temperature on bread making.

Cellular Respiration in Plants

Cells in plants and animals carry out respiration. Cellular respiration breaks down glucose to form ATP. One of the products of this reaction is carbon dioxide gas. Study the equation for cellular respiration.

$$C_6H_{12}O_6 \quad + \quad 6O_2 \quad \longrightarrow \quad 6CO_2 \quad + \quad 6H_2O \quad + \quad ATP$$

glucose   **oxygen**   **yields**   **carbon**   **water**   **ATP**
                                         dioxide

Carbon dioxide gas is colorless and odorless. It can be difficult to detect in the lab. Bromthymol blue is a chemical that reveals the presence of carbon dioxide. This chemical changes color as pH changes. Production of carbon dioxide in water changes the pH of water. When carbon dioxide dissolves in water, it forms carbonic acid. Carbonic acid makes water slightly acidic. In the lab, you will use bromthymol blue to identify respiration in plant cells.

Materials   safety goggles   2 test tubes
                      lab coat or apron   2 stoppers
                      20 mL bromthymol blue   test tube rack
                      5 germinating seeds   labels
                      5 boiled seeds

Procedure

1. Put on safety goggles and a lab coat or apron.

2. Label your test tubes A and B.

3. Pour 10 mL of bromthymol blue in each test tube. Write down the color of the bromthymol blue solution. **Safety Alerts: If you get bromthymol blue in your eyes, immediately flush with water. Avoid getting bromthymol blue on your skin or clothes because it causes stains.**

4. Place 5 germinating seeds in Test Tube A. Put a stopper in the tube.

5. Place 5 boiled seeds in Test Tube B. Put a stopper in the tube.

6. In the data table, record the color in each test tube.

7. After 24 hours, check the color in the test tubes. Record any changes in color in the data table.

Cellular Respiration in Plants, continued

Test Tube	Color at Beginning of Experiment	Color After 24 Hours
A		
B		

Cleanup/Disposal

Follow your teacher's instructions for cleanup and disposal of materials.

Analysis

1. What was the original color in Test Tube A? _____

What was the color after 24 hours? _____

2. What was the original color in Test Tube B? _____

What was the color after 24 hours? _____

Conclusions

1. Do germinating seeds produce carbon dioxide? _____

How do you know?

_____

2. Do boiled seeds produce carbon dioxide? _____

How do you know?

_____

3. How would your results change if you used more seeds
in each test tube?

_____

_____

Explore Further

Compare the rate at which different kinds of seeds release carbon dioxide.

Express Lab 8

Use with Express Lab 8, page 226

Materials   lab coat or apron
8 paper towels
tap water
10 bean seeds
2 containers, such as plastic cups or self-sealing plastic bags

Procedure

1. Put on a lab coat or apron.

2. Moisten the paper towels with tap water.

3. Put 5 bean seeds between the layers of 4 paper towels. Repeat with the other 5 bean seeds and paper towels.

4. Put each set of paper towels and seeds upright in a container.

5. Put one container in a sunny place, such as a windowsill. Put the other container in a dark, lightproof place, such as a closet.

6. After 7 days, examine the seeds. Examine the seeds again after 14 days.

Analysis

1. After 7 days, how do the two sets differ?

_____

How do they differ after 14 days?

_____

2. Describe the growth form of the seedlings raised in darkness. How is this helpful to the seedlings?

_____

_____

_____

Oxygen Production During Photosynthesis

Use with Investigation 8, pages 228–229

During photosynthesis, plants use energy from sunlight to combine carbon dioxide (CO_2) and water to make glucose. Plants release oxygen (O_2) and water. In this investigation, you will see the roles of carbon dioxide and oxygen during photosynthesis.

Materials
safety goggles
lab coat or apron
scissors
2 *Elodea* sprigs
heavy-duty thread
2 glass rods

2 large test tubes
wax pencil
0.25% sodium bicarbonate ($NaHCO_3$) solution
cooled, boiled distilled water
test tube rack
lamp

Procedure

1. Put on safety goggles and a lab coat or apron.

2. Using scissors, remove two healthy sprigs of *Elodea*. Then recut the end of each sprig at a 45° angle. **Safety Alert: Be careful when using scissors.**

3. Use two pieces of thread to tie each sprig to a glass rod.

4. With the sprig's cut side up, place each rod into a test tube.

5. With a wax pencil, label the test tubes 1 and 2. Fill Test Tube 1 with 0.25% sodium bicarbonate solution. Be sure the *Elodea* sprig is covered with the solution. Fill Test Tube 2 with boiled and cooled distilled water. Be sure the *Elodea* sprig is covered with the distilled water.

6. Place the test tubes into a test tube rack. Place rack so that the tubes are at an equal distance from the lamp. Turn the lamp on.

7. Wait 5 minutes. Then watch both *Elodea* sprigs for bubbles that form at the cut end. Then turn the lamp off.

Cleanup/Disposal

Before leaving the lab, clean up your materials and wash your hands.

Oxygen Production During Photosynthesis, continued

Analysis

1. In which test tube did bubbles appear? _____

2. What do the bubbles contain? _____

Conclusions

1. What was the role of the sodium bicarbonate solution?

_____

_____

2. Why did bubbles not appear in one of the test tubes?

_____

_____

Explore Further

Use a similar procedure to test the effect of light on photosynthesis.

Light and Photosynthesis

Use with Discovery Investigation 8, pages 236–237

Plants need light to perform photosynthesis. Does the amount of light affect the rate of photosynthesis? You will find out in this lab.

Materials
safety goggles
lab coat or apron
large flask
cool tap water
scissors
Elodea sprig
heavy-duty thread

glass rod
large test tube
0.25% sodium bicarbonate ($NaHCO_3$) solution
meterstick
lamp
stopwatch

Procedure

1. Put on safety goggles and a lab coat or apron.

2. Fill the flask with cool tap water.

3. Use scissors to cut a healthy sprig of *Elodea*. **Safety Alert: Be careful when using scissors.** Be sure the sprig will fit inside the large test tube. Recut the end of the sprig at a 45° angle. With a piece of thread, tie the sprig securely to the glass rod.

4. With the cut end up, place the glass rod into the test tube. Fill the test tube with 0.25% sodium bicarbonate solution. Be sure the *Elodea* sprig is covered with the solution.

5. Place the test tube into the flask. Place the flask 1 meter from the lamp. Turn on the lamp.

6. Wait 5 minutes. Then watch the *Elodea* sprig for bubbles that form at the cut end. Once bubbles start to appear, count the number of bubbles that form each minute. Do this for 5 minutes, recording your observations in a data table.

7. Write a hypothesis about the relationship between the amount of light and the rate of photosynthesis.

8. Write a procedure for an experiment to test your hypothesis. Include Safety Alerts. Hint: Consider using different distances between the lamp and the *Elodea* sprig.

9. Have your hypothesis and procedure approved by your teacher. Then carry out your experiment.

Light and Photosynthesis, continued

Cleanup/Disposal

Before leaving the lab, clean up your materials and wash your hands.

Analysis

1. What is the purpose of the water in the flask?

_____

2. At which distance from the light was photosynthesis greatest?

_____

Conclusions

1. Was your hypothesis supported by the results of your experiment?

_____

2. Do you think temperature affects the rate of photosynthesis? _____

Suggest an experiment that you could perform to find out.

_____

_____

Explore Further

How could you find out the effects of different colors of light on photosynthesis?

_____

_____

_____

Leaf Cross Section

Leaves are solar collectors on plants. Their primary job is to house the chloroplasts and absorb the sun's energy. Leaves are thin and flat, making it possible for carbon dioxide and water vapor to reach every cell. Openings on leaves provide passageways for the gases.

Water is transported to leaves through tube-shaped structures called vascular bundles. Each bundle resembles a group of thin straws bound together. Vascular bundles also carry glucose made in photosynthesis to the rest of the plant.

In this lab, you will examine the internal structures of a leaf. You will identify some of the leaf parts involved in photosynthesis.

Materials   prepared slide of leaf cross section
compound microscope

Procedure

1. Place a prepared slide of leaf cross section on the microscope stage. Follow your teacher's instructions for focusing the microscope. **Safety Alert: Handle the glass slide with care.**

2. Focus the microscope on low power, then on medium power.

3. Compare what you see in the microscope with the illustration of the leaf shown here or on page 225.

4. On your paper, sketch what you see under the microscope.

5. Using the illustration as a guide, label the stomata, vascular bundles, and mesophyll in your sketch.

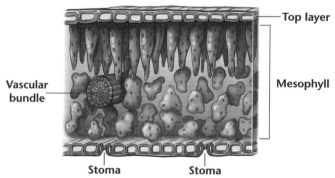

6. Two large cells called guard cells surround each stoma. Label a guard cell in your drawing.

7. The epidermis of the leaf is a layer of cells on the outer surface. Notice that the lower epidermis has more stomata than the upper. Label the upper and lower epidermis in your drawing.

8. A waxy layer covers the epidermis. This layer prevents evaporation and water loss. Label the waxy layer in your drawing.

Leaf Cross Section, continued

Cleanup/Disposal

Follow your teacher's instructions for cleanup and disposal of materials.

Analysis

1. Observe the mesophyll region of your leaf drawing. Would you describe it

as spongy or compact?_____

2. What color is the mesophyll region? _____

Conclusion

1. In what part of the leaf do you think that most of the photosynthesis
takes place: epidermis, mesophyll, or vascular bundle?
Explain your reasoning.

_____

_____

2. For photosynthesis to occur, gases must be able to circulate around
chloroplasts. How does the structure of the mesophyll assist the circulation
of oxygen and carbon dioxide?

_____

_____

3. From observing the leaf, what parts do you think protect the mesophyll?
Explain your answer.

_____

_____

Explore Further

Compare the structure of a privet (or any other dicotyledon) leaf to the structure
of a leaf or stem of a CAM plant or a C_4 plant.

Chlorophyll Chromatography

A pigment is a substance that absorbs light of certain wavelengths. Chlorophyll *a* is a pigment. It absorbs red, orange, blue, and violet wavelengths. Chlorophyll *a* reflects green and yellow wavelengths of light. Chlorophyll *a* gives plants a yellow-green color. Chlorophyll *b* reflects green and blue wavelengths of light. Carotenoids are yellow or gold because those are the wavelengths these pigments reflect.

Plants usually contain chlorophyll *b* and two or three other pigments. By having several kinds of pigments, plants are able to absorb light in every part of the light spectrum. Chromatography is a way of separating these pigments.

Materials

safety goggles	mortar and pestle
lab coat or apron	50 mL Erlenmeyer flask and stopper
1 piece of coffee filter paper	(or small jar with lid)
(or chromatography paper)	test tube
5–10 fresh spinach leaves	test tube rack
15 mL 95% ethanol	plastic wrap (enough to cover test tube)
pinch of sand	ruler
2 toothpicks	pencil
tape	scissors

Procedure

1. Put on safety goggles and a lab coat or apron.

2. Cut spinach leaves into small pieces with the scissors. **Safety Alert: Handle scissors with care.**

3. Place the leaves in the mortar and grind for one minute.

4. Add a pinch of sand and 10 mL of 95% ethanol. Continue to grind for another minute. **Safety Alert: Alcohol is flammable. Use in a well-ventilated room. Keep away from open flames.**

5. Pour the alcohol mixture into the flask and put in the stopper. Set aside for about 10 minutes.

6. Cut a narrow strip of coffee filter paper (or chromatography paper). Make the strip a little longer than the test tube.

7. Roll one end of the paper strip around the toothpick and tape in place.

8. Lower the strip of paper into the test tube until the toothpick rests across the top. Make sure that the paper does not touch the bottom of the tube.

Chlorophyll Chromatography, continued

9. Remove the toothpick and paper from the test tube.

10. Measure one to two centimeters from the free end of the strip of paper. Draw a line across the paper with the pencil.

11. With a second toothpick, transfer one small drop of the liquid part of the alcohol and spinach mixture onto the pencil line on the filter paper.

12. Pour 5 mL of 95% ethanol in the test tube.

13. Replace the filter paper and toothpick in the test tube. Cover the test tube with plastic wrap and place it in the test tube rack. Set aside for 15–20 minutes.

14. Remove the strip of filter paper from the test tube and allow it to dry.

Analysis

1. As alcohol is absorbed by the filter paper, it dissolves the pigments in the green liquid. The solvent carries these pigments up the paper. On a piece of paper, draw the appearance of the strip of filter paper. Indicate the number of bands that formed. Label the color of each band.

2. How far up the filter paper did the alcohol flow? _____

How do you know? _____

Conclusions

1. Carotenoids are yellow pigments. Because they are lightweight, they are carried farther up the paper than other pigments. Another yellow pigment, xanthophyll, cannot travel as far up the paper as carotenoid. Chlorophyll *a* makes a blue-green band and chlorophyll *b* forms a yellow-green band. Which of these bands can you see on your strip of filter paper?

_____

2. What was the original color of the spinach leaves? _____

Based on your results, which pigments combine in spinach leaves to produce that color?

_____

3. Each pigment traveled a different distance up the strip of paper. Why do you think this is?

_____

Explore Further

Use the same technique to examine the pigments in leaves that are red or yellow.

Biology: Cycles of Life

Express Lab 9

Use with Express Lab 9, page 250

Materials   20 different colored beads
2 pieces of string or twine
twist tie

Procedure

1. String together 10 beads of various colors on a piece of string or twine. To keep the beads in place, knot the ends. This is a model of a chromosome.

2. Exchange your chromosome model with another classmate. Use 10 more beads and string to create a sister chromatid for the chromosome you received.

3. Tie the sister chromatids together near the center with a twist tie.

Analysis

1. How did you create the sister chromatid?

   _____

   _____

2. What do the different colored beads represent? What does the twist tie represent?

   _____

   _____

3. In which stage of interphase are sister chromatids created?

   _____

Whitefish Mitosis

In multicellular organisms, mitosis provides new cells for growth. Cells in plants, animals, and fungi go through the process of mitosis. In one-celled organisms, the method of reproduction is a process called binary fission.

In this lab, you will observe the cells of a whitefish in the process of mitosis.

Materials   safety goggles
              lab coat or apron
              prepared slides of whitefish blastula in mitosis
              microscope

Procedure

1. Put on safety goggles and a lab coat or apron.

2. Examine one of the prepared slides of mitosis in whitefish blastula. **Safety Alert: Handle glass microscope slides with care. Dispose of broken glass properly.**

3. Make a sketch of a cell. Label your drawing as *interphase, prophase, metaphase, anaphase,* or *telophase.*

4. Examine another prepared slide of mitosis in whitefish blastula. Sketch what you see. Label the drawing as *interphase, prophase, metaphase, anaphase,* or *telophase.*

5. Repeat Steps 3 and 4 until you have examined and drawn cells in all five phases of mitosis.

Cleanup/Disposal

Follow your teacher's instructions for cleanup and disposal of materials.

Analysis

1. Describe the appearance of the chromatids in the whitefish mitosis slides.

   _____

   _____

2. How does a cell in interphase look?

   _____

3. What happens to a whitefish cell after telophase?

   _____

Whitefish Mitosis, continued

Conclusions

1. Whitefish are animals. What is the difference between an animal cell in mitosis and a plant cell, like onion root tip, in mitosis?

   _____

   _____

2. What characteristics do plant and animal cells in mitosis share?

   _____

   _____

Explore Further

Compare whitefish blastula cells to nonmitotic cells scraped from human cheeks.

Observing Cell Cycle Phases

Use with Investigation 9, pages 254–255

Cells grow during interphase. They also make copies of their DNA and organelles during this phase. Cells reproduce to make new cells during mitosis and cytokinesis. As cells enter mitosis, they separate the DNA copies. During cytokinesis, the cell grows larger and divides in two. Making new cells allows an organism to grow larger or replace damaged cells. In this investigation, you will examine the cells of an onion root. You will observe cells in different phases of the cell cycles.

Materials   safety goggles
                lab coat or apron
                prepared slide of onion root
                microscope

Procedure

1. Put on safety goggles and a lab coat or apron.

2. Examine the prepared slide of an onion root. **Safety Alert: Handle glass microscope slides with care. Dispose of broken glass properly.**

3. Find a cell in interphase. On a sheet of paper, draw what you observe. Label the parts of the cell that you recognize.

4. Find examples of cells in mitosis. Draw examples of a cell in prophase, metaphase, anaphase, telophase, and cytokinesis. Label the cell parts you recognize.

Cleanup/Disposal

When you are finished, return the prepared slide to your teacher.

Analysis

1. What cell parts were you able to identify easily?

_____

_____

Observing Cell Cycle Phases, continued

2. What cell parts were difficult or impossible to identify?

_____

_____

Conclusions

1. How did you recognize a cell in interphase?

_____

_____

2. What were the main characteristics of the cells in mitosis?

_____

_____

3. How did you identify a cell undergoing cytokinesis?

_____

_____

Explore Further

In which phase were most of the cells you observed? What can you infer about
the life of a cell from this observation?

_____

_____

_____

_____

Stages of Mitosis Flip Chart

During most of its life, a cell is in interphase. When it is time to reproduce, a cell makes copies of its organelles and chromosomes. During mitosis, these structures separate into two new cells. Each new cell is exactly like the original. In this activity, you will create a flipchart that describes what happens during mitosis.

Materials   3 sheets of paper
pen or pencil
markers, paints, or crayons
stapler

Procedure

1. Arrange the three sheets of paper into a flip chart. See Figure A.

Figure A
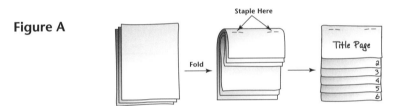

Fold the stack over so that the edges of the top and bottom halves are staggered. Staple the stack along the top. You have created a flip chart. You will draw and describe the stages of mitosis on this flip chart.

2. The top page is the title page. Decide on a name for your flip chart and write it on the title page.

3. On the second page, draw a cell in prophase. Use Figure 9.1.1 on page 249 in the student text as a guide. Below the drawing, describe the events of prophase.

4. On the third page, draw a cell in metaphase. Describe the events of metaphase.

5. On the fourth page, draw a cell in anaphase. Describe the events of anaphase.

6. On the fifth page, draw a cell in telophase. Describe the events of telophase.

7. On the sixth page, summarize the process of mitosis. Include a sentence that describes the purpose of mitosis.

Cleanup/Disposal

Follow your teacher's instructions for cleanup and disposal of materials.

Stages of Mitosis Flip Chart, continued

Analysis

1. What are the four phases of mitosis?

_____

_____

2. When do two sets of sister chromatids form?

_____

3. Why do cells make sister chromataids?

_____

Conclusions

1. In what kinds of plant tissues would you expect to find cells that are in mitosis? Explain your answer.

_____

_____

2. In what kinds of animal tissues would you expect to find cells in mitosis? Explain your answer.

_____

_____

3. What is the function of mitosis?

_____

Explore Further

Create a flip chart showing the events of meiosis.

Modeling the Movement of Chromosomes

Use with Discovery Investigation 9, pages 269–270

DNA is organized into sections called chromosomes. Each chromosome contains many genes. Human chromosomes come in pairs, with one chromosome coming from each parent. The genes on a chromosome are mixed and distributed during meiosis. In meiosis I, chromosomes trade genetic information by crossing over. In meiosis II, the chromosome pairs are separated and redistributed in gametes.

In this investigatoin, you will create models of chromosomes with different-colored clay. You will use your models to show how meiosis I and meiosis II cause genes to mix, creating different chromosomes.

Materials   lab coat or apron
modeling clay in different colors

Procedure

1. Form small groups. Select either meiosis I or meiosis II to model.

2. Put on a lab coat or apron.

3. Use the modeling clay to design and create chromosome models. Determine the size and color of your models. Keep your models simple.

4. On paper, diagram the process your group wants to model (meiosis I or meiosis II). Label the activities that occur during each phase of the process.

5. Now use your chromosome models to show each phase of the process. Show how the chromosomes move or change. Use different clay colors to make this clear.

6. Compare the models your group created with the models of other groups. Compare how each group showed that the genes on their chromosomes have moved.

Cleanup/Disposal

When you are finished, return any unused modeling clay to the proper place. Wash your hands in warm, soapy water.

Modeling the Movement of Chromosomes, continued

Analysis

1. Compare your models with models of the same process created by another group. How do the two sets differ?

_____

_____

_____

2. Compare your models with models of a different process created by another group. How different are the two sets?

_____

_____

_____

Conclusions

1. In meiosis I, how does the size of the chromosome and the site of crossing over affect the number and type of genes that are transferred? Are some genes more likely to be transferred in crossing over than others?

_____

_____

_____

2. Suppose one of the groups modeling meiosis II used chromosomes that had crossed over in meiosis I as their starting materials. How would this affect offspring?

_____

_____

_____

Explore Further

Compare the models of the gamete cells from the end of meiosis II with another group's gamete cells. How much does this affect offspring?

_____

_____

_____

Express Lab 10

Use with Express Lab 10, page 283

Materials   safety goggles
2 coins

Procedure

1. Put on safety goggles.

2. Probability is the likelihood that a specific event will occur.
Toss a coin into the air. What is the probability that the coin
will land head up? Tail up?   _____

3. Toss the second coin. Does the way that the first coin landed
affect how the second coin landed?   _____

4. What is the probability that both coins will land head up?
To find out, multiply the separate probabilities of each event. _____

Analysis

1. How is each coin toss similar to an allele?

_____

_____

2. How can you use a Punnett square to show your results?

_____

_____

Using Punnett Squares

Use with Investigation 10, pages 290–291

A Punnett square is a tool used to predict the possible offspring of a cross. In a Punnett square, a capital letter stands for a dominant allele. A lowercase letter stands for a recessive allele. Each parent carries two alleles. If the parent is true breeding, the alleles are the same. In this investigation, you will use Punnett squares to predict the offspring of genetic crosses.

Materials   paper
pencil

Procedure

1. In pea plants, a flower color of purple is dominant over the color white. Use capital *P* to stand for the allele for purple. Use a lowercase *p* to stand for the allele for white. In his experiments, Mendel crossed a true-breeding purple-flowering plant with a true-breeding white-flowering plant. On a sheet of paper, write the symbols for these two parental (P-generation) plants.

2. Draw a Punnett square like the one shown below. Separate and write each of the alleles from one parent in the indicated spaces along the top. Separate and write each allele from the other parent along the side. Fill in the four boxes in the Punnett square. Each box shows the F_1 combination of the allele from one parent (along the top) with the allele from the other parent (along the side).

3. Draw a new Punnett square. Cross two F_1 plants with each other. The new Punnett square will show the resulting F_2 individuals.

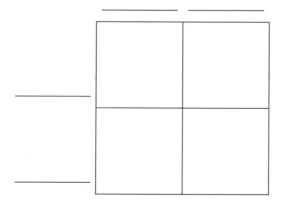

Using Punnett Squares, continued

Analysis

1. What allele combinations and flower colors are possible among the F_1 plants?

_____

_____

2. What allele combinations are possible among the F_2 plants?

_____

What flower colors are possible?

_____

Write the ratios of combinations and flower colors in this generation.

_____

_____

Conclusions

1. Why did Mendel use true-breeding plants for each parental cross?

_____

_____

2. Write a new question about genetic crosses that you could explore in another investigation.

_____

_____

Explore Further

Use the procedure above to show the offspring of a dihybrid cross.

Probability of Gender

The gender of an offspring is determined by sex chromosomes. The male parent contributes two different sex chromosomes: an X and a Y. The female parent supplies two of the same sex chromosome: two X's.

The probability that an offspring will be male or female can be determined. Probability is the chance or possibility that something will occur. In this lab, you will determine the probability that any offspring will be male or female.

Materials   safety goggles   notebook   2 pennies
lab coat or apron   pen or pencil   masking tape
calculator

Procedure

1. Put on safety goggles and a lab coat or apron.

2. Put masking tape on both sides of both pennies.

3. Write X on both sides of one penny. This penny represents the female sex chromosomes.

4. On the other penny, write X on one side and Y on the other side. This penny represents the male sex chromosomes.

5. Flip the two coins. When the pennies land, examine them. If the combination is XX, place a mark in the XX column of the data table. If the combination is XY, place a mark in the XY column.

6. Repeat step 5 nine more times. Record the combinations in the data table.

7. Determine the percentage of XX combinations after 10 flips. To do so, use your calculator to divide the number of XX by 10, then multiply by 100.

$$\text{percentage of XX} = \frac{\text{number of XX}}{\text{total number of flips}} \times 100$$

Record this percentage. _____

Coin flip number	XX	XY
1		
2		
3		
4		
5		
6		
7		
8		
9		
10		

Probability of Gender, continued

8. Determine the percentage of XY after 10 flips. To do so, use your calculator to divide the number of XY by 10, then multiply by 100.

$$\text{percentage of XY} = \frac{\text{number of XY}}{\text{total number of flips}} \times 100$$

Record this percentage. _____

9. Create a data table where you can record the results of 50 flips.

10. Flip the coins 50 times, and record the results of each flip in your data table.

11. Use the formula in step 7 to determine the percentage of XXs after 50 flips.

12. Use the formula in step 8 to determine the percentage of XYs after 50 flips.

Cleanup/Disposal

Follow your teacher's instructions for cleanup and disposal of materials.

Analysis

1. In the first 10 flips, what percentage of offspring had an XX combination? _____

An XY combination? _____

2. After 50 flips, what percentage of offspring had an XX combination? _____

An XY combination? _____

Conclusions

1. If a couple has four daughters, what are the chances that their next child will be a boy? Explain your answer.

_____

_____

2. Fifty coin flips gives you a larger sample size than ten coin flips. In which case was the probability of XX closer to 50 percent? Explain your answer.

_____

3. Complete the following Punnett square. It predicts the chances that an offspring will be male or female. What do the results of the Punnett square tell you?

	X	Y
X		
X		

_____

Explore Further

Compare results of 50 tosses to the results of 100 tosses.

Traits Depend on Chromosomes

Brown eye color (B) is dominant over blue eye color (b). In this lab, you will find out the possible genotypes and phenotypes of offspring. Brown pipe cleaners represent genes for brown eyes. Blue pipe cleaners represent genes for blue eyes.

Materials   safety goggles
               lab coat or apron
               4 brown pipe cleaners
               4 blue pipe cleaners
               2 small paper bags

Procedure

1. Put on safety goggles and a lab coat or apron.

2. Label one paper bag as "Father." Label the other paper bag as "Mother."

3. Place four brown pipe cleaners in Father's paper bag. Each pipe cleaner represents a chromosome that carries a gene (B) for brown eye color.

4. Place four blue pipe cleaners in Mother's paper bag. Each pipe cleaner represents a chromosome that carries a gene (b) for blue eye color.

5. Remove one chromosome from Father's bag and place it on the desktop. Remove one chromosome from Mother's bag and place it beside the Father's chromosome. These two chromosomes represent the gene combination of 25 percent of the offspring of Father and Mother. Write this gene combination in the data table in the column called "First drawing." Indicate whether the offspring would have blue eyes or brown eyes.

	First Drawing:	Second Drawing:	Third Drawing:	Fourth Drawing:
Father's gene				
Mother's gene				
Eye color of offspring with these genes				

Traits Depend on Chromosomes, continued

6. Remove another chromosome from Father's bag and place it on the desk. Remove a chromosome from Mother's bag and place it beside father's. This represents the gene combination of another 25 percent of the offspring. Write this gene combination in the data table.

7. Repeat step 6 until all of the chromosomes have been paired.

8. Repeat the activity, but change the parents' genes. Give Father two brown pipe cleaners and two blue pipe cleaners. Give Mother two brown pipe cleaners and two blue pipe cleaners. Determine the possible gene combinations. Create a data table and name it "Gene combinations of the second cross."

Cleanup/Disposal

Follow your teacher's instructions for cleanup and disposal of materials.

Analysis

1. In the first cross is the Father heterozygous or homozygous for brown eyes? _____

2. Write the Mother's genotype in the first cross. _____

What is the Mother's phenotype? _____

Conclusions

1. What is the eye color of offspring of the first cross? _____

2. What is the eye color of offspring of the second cross? _____

3. How are these two genetic crosses similar to the work of Gregor Mendel?

_____

Explore Further

Perform a dihybrid cross by creating two sacks for Father and two sacks for Mother.

Interpreting Pedigrees

Use with Discovery Investigation 10, pages 297–298

A pedigree is a chart that traces a family's genetic history for a certain trait. In this lab, you will learn how to interpret a pedigree.

Materials   paper
                 pencil

Procedure

1. On a sheet of paper, copy the pedigree shown below. Circles represent females. Squares represent males. A horizontal line between a male and a female represents marriage. A vertical line that comes down from a married couple leads to their children. A Roman numeral indicates each generation.

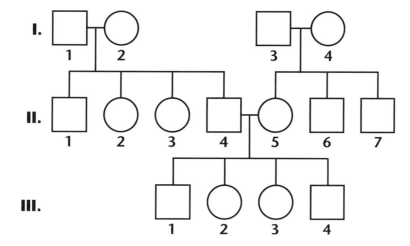

2. Read the following information. It applies to the pedigree in Step 1.

- Attached earlobes are attached to the side of the head. Free earlobes are not attached to the side of the head. Persons I-3 and I-4 have free earlobes. So does their son, II-7. Their daughter, II-5, and son, II-6, have attached earlobes. Their daughter's husband, II-4, also has attached earlobes.

- Person I-1 has type A blood. His wife, I-2, has type B blood. They have four children: son II-1 (type O), daughter II-2 (type AB), daughter II-3 (type A), and son II-4 (type B).

3. Write a procedure describing how you could determine the possible phenotypes and genotypes of the Generation III individuals.

4. Have your procedure approved by your teacher. Write the possible phenotypes and genotypes for Generation III.

Interpreting Pedigrees, continued

Analysis

1. Write the phenotypes and genotypes of the persons described in Step 2.

_____

_____

2. Which two persons are adopted?

_____

Conclusions

1. Is either the earlobe trait or the blood type trait a sex-linked trait? Explain your answer.

_____

_____

_____

2. What are the possible phenotypes and genotypes for Generation III?

_____

_____

_____

Explore Further

How can a pedigree reveal a child's risk of inheriting a genetic disease?

_____

_____

Express Lab 11

Use with Express Lab 11, page 308

Materials paper
         pen

Procedure

Erwin Chargraff analyzed the amounts of nitrogenous bases in the DNA of various organisms. Some of his results are shown in the table below.

Organism	Adenine	Guanine	Cystosine	Thymine
human	30.4%	19.6%	19.9%	30.1%
ox	29.0%	21.2%	21.2%	28.7%
sea urchin	32.8%	17.7%	17.3%	32.1%

Analysis

1. Which nitrogenous bases are single-ringed bases?

_____

Which are double-ringed bases?

_____

2. How do Chargraff's results vary? What do his results suggest about DNA?

_____

_____

_____

Modeling DNA

Use with Investigation 11, pages 314–315

DNA is made of two strands of nucleotides arranged in the form of a double helix. Each nucleotide is made of a sugar called deoxyribose, a phosphate group, and one of four nitrogenous bases.

Materials   safety goggles   large sheet of paper
                  lab coat or apron   tape
                  paper models for sugar, phosphate group,   wooden craft sticks
                      cytosine (C), thymine (T), adenine (A),   ruler
                      guanine (G)

Procedure

1. Put on safety goggles and a lab coat or apron.

2. Place a large sheet of paper on your desk. The paper represents the width of a DNA molecule.

3. Select a model of a deoxyribose and a model of a phosphate group. Position them along one side of the paper. Show how they form the sugar-phosphate backbone of one strand of the double helix. Tape them to the paper.

4. Select two nitrogenous bases for your first base pair. Follow the rules of complementary base pairing. Tape one base to the sugar of one strand. Tape the second base to the other sugar.

5. Position wooden craft sticks to represent hydrogen bonds between the bases. **Safety Alert: Broken craft sticks may have sharp edges. Do not use them.**

6. Select another sugar model and phosphate group model. Position them along the other side of the paper. They represent the second side of the sugar-phosphate backbone of the second strand. Be sure the sugars are directly across from each other. Then tape down the models to the paper.

7. Repeat Steps 2 to 6, adding two more nitrogenous bases to your DNA molecule.

8. Use a ruler to measure the widths of the two sets of base pairs in your model. Record your data.

Cleanup/Disposal

When you are finished, put away the tape and ruler.

Modeling DNA, continued

Analysis

1. Are the two sets of base pairs in your model equal in width? Explain your answer.

_____

_____

_____

2. Which nitrogenous bases can be correctly paired?

_____

_____

Conclusions

1. A DNA double helix is the same width throughout. What does this suggest about base pairing?

_____

_____

_____

2. Write a new question about DNA structure that you could explore in another investigation.

_____

_____

_____

Explore Further

Combine your finished model with other students' models to create a longer double helix.

Extracting DNA

DNA is found in the cells of living things. To study the molecule, scientists extract it from cells. DNA is used to identify a person since no two people have the same genetic material. It is also used to find out if people are related. In this lab, you will extract DNA.

Materials

safety goggles
lab coat or apron
DNA source ($\frac{1}{2}$ cup of
one of the following:
   split peas, onion, spinach,
   chicken liver, calf thymus,
   or wheat germ)
2 cups ice cold water
pinch of salt (less than $\frac{1}{8}$
   teaspoon)

pinch of meat tenderizer
   (less than $\frac{1}{8}$ teaspoon)
2 tablespoons liquid dish
   washing detergent
10 mL ice cold 95% ethyl
   alcohol
blender
teaspoon
tablespoon
measuring cup

test tube
graduated cylinder
200 mL beaker
strainer
stirring rod
wooden stick (about the
   size of a stirring rod) or
   swab

Procedure

1. Put on safety goggles and a lab coat or apron.

2. Place $\frac{1}{2}$ cup of your DNA source, a pinch of salt, and 2 cups of ice cold water in the blender. Blend on high for 10 to 20 seconds. The blender and salt separate the cells in your DNA source. **Safety Alert: Handle glass materials with care. Dispose of broken glass properly.**

3. Position the strainer over the 200 mL beaker. Pour the contents of the blender into the strainer. Give the liquid a few minutes to drip through the strainer and collect in the beaker. The liquid in the beaker contains the cells. Discard the material in the strainer.

4. Add about 2 tablespoons liquid dishwashing detergent to the liquid in the beaker. With the stirring rod, stir very gently. Let the liquid stand for 5 to 10 minutes. The dishwashing liquid breaks down the cell and nuclear membranes.

5. Fill a test tube $\frac{1}{3}$ full of the liquid from the beaker.

6. Add a pinch of meat tenderizer to the liquid in the test tube. Stir the mixture very gently so that you do not damage the strands of DNA. The enzymes in meat tenderizer break apart the proteins that wrap around DNA.

Extracting DNA, continued

7. Tilt the test tube and slowly add 2 or 3 milliliters of cold alcohol so that it forms a layer on top of the liquid.

8. DNA will form a white, stringy mass at the place where the liquid and alcohol meet. Use a wooden stick or swab to gently scoop out the DNA.

Cleanup/Disposal

Follow your teacher's instructions for cleanup and disposal of materials.

Analysis

1. What did you use as a source of DNA?

_____

2. Where is the DNA in living things located?

_____

3. What is the purpose of breaking the cell and nuclear membranes in Step 4?

_____

Conclusions

1. How does DNA carry a cell's genetic information?

_____

2. What are the parts of a DNA molecule?

_____

Explore Further

Extract DNA from another source. Compare the amount of DNA produced by the first and second sources.

Crime Scene DNA

DNA from a crime scene can be compared to the DNA of a suspect. If a match is found, the suspect can be prosecuted. To analyze DNA, scientists use enzymes called restriction endonucleases. These break the long strands into smaller pieces. Scientists can compare the small pieces produced in two or more different DNA samples.

In this lab, you will study four fake DNA samples. One is from a crime scene. Three are from suspects. Your goal is to find out if any of the suspects' DNA matches the crime scene DNA. You will pretend to cut the DNA with a restriction endonuclease. Then you will examine the cut pieces. In this model, the enzyme you use cuts DNA at this base sequence: CCTAAT.

Materials   Figure A
scissors
2 sheets of $8\frac{1}{2}$" x 11" paper

Figure A. DNA from the crime scene and three suspects.

Crime Scene

TATTCGAACCTAATTTTAATAGGGGCACGGGCCCCTAATCCCCATATAGAGGT

Suspect 1

AACCTAATCATATTTTTTTGAGAGAAAAGGGG CCTAATAAAGCCCATAGGGGC

Suspect 2

CCTAATCCCCATATAGAGGTCCTAATTATTCGAACCTAATTTTAATAGGGGCACGGGCC

Suspect 3

GGCTTAACCTTAACCCCACACACAGGGGGTTTCCTAATCCCCAATTTAGCCCAAAGAT

Crime Scene DNA, continued

Procedure

1. Make a copy of the table on your paper. Use the table to organize the DNA samples.

Crime Scene	Suspect 1
Suspect 2	Suspect 3

2. Trace or draw each of the four samples in Figure A on the other sheet of paper. You will cut out the items on that sheet.

3. Use scissors to cut out the DNA from the crime scene sample. **Safety Alert: Handle scissors with care.** Examine the sequence of bases in the sample carefully. Every time you find the sequence CCTAAT in the sample, underline it.

4. With scissors, cut out the sequences you underlined. Discard these sequences.

5. Arrange the remaining pieces of DNA in the table under "Crime Scene." Stack samples in the column. Place the smallest piece at the top of the column and the largest piece at the bottom. Tape the pieces to the paper.

6. Cut out the suspect 1 DNA sample. Examine the sequence of bases carefully. Underline each CCTAAT sequence. Cut out and discard these sequences.

7. Arrange the remaining pieces of the suspect 1 DNA sample in the table under "Suspect 1."

8. Repeat Steps 3 and 4 for Suspect 2 DNA and Suspect 3 DNA samples. Place each sample in the table.

9. Compare the crime scene DNA to the DNA from each suspect.

Cleanup/Disposal

Follow your teacher's instructions for cleanup and disposal of materials.

Crime Scene DNA, continued

Analysis

1. Do any of the suspects have DNA just like the DNA from the crime scene? _____

    If so, which suspect? _____

2. What is the job of a restriction endonuclease?

    _____

Conclusions

1. DNA is found in every cell. Suggest two ways that a suspect could leave DNA at a crime scene.

    _____

    _____

2. How does the use of a restriction endonuclease help analyze DNA?

    _____

    _____

3. Explain how DNA can be used to identify a suspect.

    _____

    _____

Explore Further

Examine a sample of real DNA that has been separated by gel electrophoresis.

A Faulty Protein

Use with Discovery Investigation 11, pages 330–331

The nucleic acid DNA contains the directions for making proteins. A mutation is a change in the sequence of DNA nucleotides. In this investigation, you will learn how a mutation can affect a blood protein called hemoglobin, causing sickle-cell disease.

Materials   paper
                  pencil

Procedure

1. Write the following DNA nucleotide sequence on a sheet of paper: **T G A G G A C T C C T C.**

2. Write the complementary mRNA sequence.

3. Table 11.1 shows the possible codons in mRNA. Each codon, or set of three nucleotide bases, codes for one amino acid. Use this table to translate the mRNA sequence in Step 2. Write the amino acid sequence that the mRNA sequence will produce.

4. Write the following DNA nucleotide sequence: **T G A G G A C A C C T C.**

   Does the DNA sequence match the one in Step 3? _____

Analysis

1. In Step 2, what is the complementary mRNA sequence? How many codons does it contain?

   _____

   _____

   _____

2. In Step 3, what is the amino acid that the mRNA sequence will produce?

   _____

   _____

3. In Step 4, what is the complementary mRNA sequence for the DNA sequence? _____
   What is the amino acid sequence that this mRNA sequence produces?

   _____

   _____

   _____

A Faulty Protein, continued

Conclusions

1. What process is occurring in Step 2?

_____

_____

2. What process is occurring in Step 3?

_____

_____

3. Identify the DNA mutation shown in Step 4. What kind of mutation is this?

_____

_____

Explore Further

When might a genetic mutation fail to affect a protein?

_____

Change the DNA sequence in Step 1 to show how a gene can undergo a mutation and still produce a normal protein.

_____

_____

_____

Table 11.1 Codons in mRNA				
First Base	Second Base			Third Base
	U	C	A	G	
U	UUU } Phenylalanine UUC UUA } Leucine UUG	UCU UCC Serine UCA UCG	UAU } Tyrosine UAC UAA } Stop UAG	UGU } Cysteine UGC UGA } Stop UGG } Tryptophan	U C A G
C	CUU CUC Leucine CUA CUG	CCU CCC Proline CCA CCG	CAU } Histidine CAC CAA } Glutamine CAG	CGU CGC Arginine CGA CGG	U C A G
A	AUU } AUC } Isolecine AUA } AUG } Start	ACU ACC Threonine ACA ACG	AAU } Asparagine AAC AAA } Lysine AAG	AGU } Serine AGC AGA } Arginine AGG	U C A G
G	GUU GUC Valine GUA GUG	GCU GCC Alanine GCA GCG	GAU } Aspartic GAC } acid GAA } Glutamic GAG } acid	GGU GGC Cysteine GGA GGG	U C A G

Express Lab 12

Use with Express Lab 12, page 346

Materials   Food products with nutrition labels

Procedure

1. Study the food labels of two different types of food.

2. Look at the ingredients list on each label. Note the amount of fiber in each type of food.

Analysis

1. What is the connection between cellulose and fiber?

   _____

   _____

2. How much fiber is recommended each day as part of a healthy diet?

   _____

3. Why is fiber important to a healthy diet?

   _____

   _____

Blood Cells

Blood is a form of connective tissue. It contains several types of blood cells that are suspended in plasma. The cells in blood can be examined under the microscope. A slide of a blood smear shows red blood cells, white blood cells, and platelets.

Materials   prepared slide of human blood
microscope

Procedure

1. Place the prepared slide of human blood on the microscope stage. Focus on high power.

2. Examine the red cells. Draw one of the red cells in your notebook.

3. Survey the slide for white blood cells. They are larger than red blood cells. The nuclei of white blood cells may be purple in color. Draw two different white blood cells.

4. Look for tiny pieces of cells. These are platelets. Draw two platelets.

Cleanup/Disposal

Follow your teacher's instructions for cleanup and disposal of materials.

Analysis

1. What kinds of cells are the most numerous: Red blood cells, white blood cells, or platelets? _____

2. Were all of the red blood cells similar in size and shape? _____

    Were the white blood cells similar in size and shape? _____

Blood Cells, continued

Conclusions

1. Do the red blood cells have nuclei? _____

2. Describe two differences in the structures of red and white blood cells.

_____

_____

3. Explain the jobs of red blood cells, white blood cells, and platelets.

_____

_____

Explore Further

Compare the cells in human blood to cells in a frog's blood.

How Exercise Affects Heart Rate

Use with Investigation 12, pages 357–358

Heart rate is usually measured by taking a person's pulse. Each time your heart beats, it sends blood rushing through your arteries. The arteries stretch a little as blood rushes through them. You can feel this stretching as a small bump or beat at a pressure point. The easiest pressure points to use are on your neck or the inside of your wrist. By counting the beats, you will find your heart rate, or pulse rate. In this lab, you will find out how your heart rate changes with exercise.

Materials   clock with a second hand

                  graph paper

Procedure

1. To record your observations, draw a table like the one shown below on a sheet of graph paper.

2. To find your resting heart rate, take your pulse. To do this, sit quietly in a chair for two minutes. Then place your first two fingers on your inner wrist near the base of your thumb. Press lightly to feel your pulse. If you do not feel a pulse, move your fingers around a little until you do.

3. Watching the second hand on a clock, count the beats you feel for exactly one minute. Record this number in your table.

Activity	Heart Rate
Sitting quietly	
After running for 1 minute	
After resting for 2 minutes	
After resting for 3 minutes	
After resting for 4 minutes	
After resting for 5 minutes	

4. Run in place for one minute. **Safety Alert: Tell your teacher if you should not do this physical activity.**

5. Immediately measure your heart rate for one minute. Record this information.

How Exercise Affects Heart Rate, continued

6. Sit quietly for one minute. Measure your heart rate for one minute. Repeat until you have recorded five measurements after you run.

7. On graph paper, make a graph from your data to show how your heart rate changed before, during, and after exercise.

Analysis

1. How did exercise affect your heart rate?

_____

_____

2. What happened to your heart rate when you stopped exercising and rested?

_____

Conclusions

1. What needs do you think your heart responded to when your heart rate changed?

_____

_____

2. What do you think heart rate tells you about the level of exercise you are performing?

_____

_____

_____

Explore Further

Measure your heart rate for one minute while you are running in place. At the same time, have a partner measure your respiration rate (the number of breaths you take per minute). How are respiration rate and heart rate related?

_____

_____

_____

_____

Examining the Body Systems of a Grasshopper

Insects have body systems similar to those of humans. Like people, insects have blood that moves in a circulatory system. A brain and network of nerves control the insect body. Food is handled in the digestive system. Oxygen enters the body through the respiratory system. Wastes are removed in the excretory system.

Insects do not have internal skeletons like people. Their bodies are covered with a hard exoskeleton. It protects the organs and supports the body.

In this lab, you will dissect a grasshopper and examine some of its body systems. The term "dissect" does not mean to cut. It means to expose to view. As you dissect, do as little cutting as possible. When using scissors, point the tips upwards to avoid cutting the structures beneath. Before cutting, lift the structure with forceps so you can see what you are doing.

Materials   safety goggles   dissecting tray   eyedropper
                        lab coat or apron   scissors   small beaker of water
                        gloves   probe
                        preserved grasshopper   forceps

Procedure

1. Put on safety goggles, a lab coat or apron, and gloves.

2. Place a preserved grasshopper in the dissecting tray.

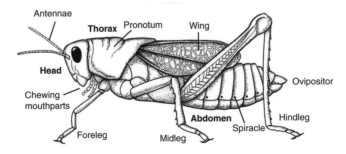

3. Compare the external features of the grasshopper to Figure 1. Identify the following parts: head, thorax, abdomen, two pairs of wings, three pairs of legs, one pair of antennae, two compound eyes, and three simple eyes.

4. Examine the first segment of the abdomen. Look under the wing for the oval tympanium. This is a membrane that acts like an eardrum. Also locate the spiracles on the sides of the abdomen. Spiracles are tubes that take in air.

Examining the Body Systems of a Grasshopper, continued

5. Use scissors to remove the wings and legs. **Safety Alert: Take care when working with scissors.**

6. Use scissors to cut along the middle of each side. Cut from the head-end toward the abdomen-end.

7. Carefully remove the top portion of the exoskeleton. Use the probe to separate the exoskeleton from the muscles and organs beneath.

8. With the eyedropper, put a few drops of water on the muscles and organs. This will keep them from drying out.

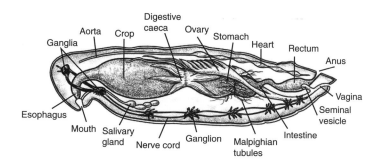

9. Look for a sac-like structure in the thorax. This is actually two organs. The head end of the sac is the crop, which stores food. The abdomen end is the muscular gizzard, which grinds food.

10. In front of the crop is a short esophagus. Find the esophagus and follow it to the mouth. Gently push the crop aside so you can look under it for the salivary glands.

11. The stomach is shaped like a sac and found behind the gizzard. Where the gizzard joins the stomach, several finger-like gastric caeca extend in both directions. They help the body absorb nutrients from food.

12. The intestine is a tube that extends from the stomach. Locate the intestine and follow it to the rectum and anus.

13. Look at the place where the stomach and intestine meet. Thread-like structures in this area are Malphigian tubules. They are the excretory organs of insects.

14. Small, white tubes in the abdomen are the trachea. They connect to the external spiracles.

15. A thin, thread-like blood vessel lies on top of the organs. This is the aorta. Follow the aorta to the abdomen until you find areas where it bulges. These bulges in the aorta are the hearts.

Examining the Body Systems of a Grasshopper, continued

16. Reproductive organs are located above the stomach and intestine. Identify the reproductive organs in the grasshopper.

17. Use scissors to carefully remove the digestive tract. Examine the body cavity to find the nerve cord. It runs along the lower surface of the body.

18. Follow the nerve cord to the brain. The brain is located between the two compound eyes.

Cleanup/Disposal

Follow your teacher's instructions for cleanup and disposal of materials.

Analysis

1. What are the three main body segments of a grasshopper?

_____

_____

2. Why is the external surface of a grasshopper hard?

_____

_____

3. What kinds of sensory organs did you find on the grasshopper's body?

_____

_____

Conclusions

1. How are body systems in the grasshopper similar to those in humans?

_____

_____

2. How are body systems in the grasshopper different from those in humans?

_____

_____

Explore Further

Use a dissecting microscope to closely examine the structures of the grasshopper.

Constructing Models of Human Joints

Use with Discovery Investigation 12, pages 379–380

The human skeletal system uses three types of joints that allow movement. The ball-and-socket joint allows rotation. The hinge joint moves back and forth in one direction. The pivot joint allows limited rotation. Together these joints allow the human skeleton to move in many different ways.

In this investigation, you will be given a variety of materials to make your own models of these joints.

Materials   safety goggles
lab coat or apron
assorted materials to model joints such as screws,
    washers, hinges, ball-like lollipops, bottle caps, craft sticks,
    pipe cleaners, modeling clay, push pins, glue

Procedure

1. In a small group, write a procedure with Safety Alerts to make one type of joint. Write the procedure as if you were giving directions to another person.

2. Put on safety goggles and a lab coat or apron.

3. Follow your procedure to construct the model. **Safety Alert: Be careful when working with materials that have sharp edges.**

Cleanup/Disposal

When you are finished, clean up your area and put extra materials away.

Analysis

1. What factors did you consider when making your joint?

_____

_____

_____

Constructing Models of Human Joints, continued

2. Where is your joint located in the human body?

_____

_____

3. What are the limitations of your joint model?

_____

_____

Conclusions

1. Describe how your joint model is different from the body joint it represents.

_____

_____

_____

2. What limitations did you have with the materials?

_____

_____

_____

3. What are the advantages of body joints compared to mechanical joints?

_____

_____

_____

Explore Further

Add a motor or pulley system to make your model move. Try to mimic the movements of the body joint. Be creative in your materials and methods.

Chapter 13

Express Lab 13

Use with Express Lab 13, page 393

Materials   marker
             3 flat sponges

Procedure

1. Form small groups.

2. Using a marker, make a shape like an X, □, or ○ on the long
side of each sponge. Make each mark different. The marks represent fossils.
The sponges represent layers of rock.

3. Put the sponges on top of each other so that the fossils face you. Observe the order
of fossils from top to bottom.

4. Hold the layers of sponges tightly on both ends. Moving your hands toward
each other, push inward against the sponges. Observe what happens to the order
of fossils from top to bottom.

Analysis

1. Which fossil is the oldest in Step 3? _____

2. How did the order of fossils change in Step 4?

_____

3. What does a scientist need to know about the rock to tell if one fossil is older
than another fossil?

_____

_____

Dinosaur Tracks

Some fossils are made of pieces of organisms that lived in the past. Paleontologists have found the skeletons of entire dinosaurs buried in sedimentary rock. Other fossils are traces of organisms, like tracks left in the mud.

A track is the impression of a foot. Several tracks may indicate an animal's path or trail. Tracks can provide information about the animals that left them. They may give clues as to the animal's age, speed, size, and behavior.

In this lab, you will analyze several sets of tracks.

Materials   safety goggles
lab coat or apron
outdoor area of sand or soft soil
yardstick
rake
Figure A

Procedure

1. Put on safety goggles and a lab coat or apron.

2. Work in groups of four or five. Ask the shortest member of your group to be "Dinosaur A." Ask the tallest member to be "Dinosaur B."

3. Measure the height of Dinosaur A. Record that height in the data table.

4. Ask Dinosaur A to walk across the sand or soft soil that has been raked clear of other marks.

5. Measure the stride of Dinosaur A's footprints. The stride is the distance from the toe of one track to the heel of the next track. Record this measurement in the data table.

6. Measure the length of one track. Record the length in the data table.

7. Measure the depth of the heel in one track. Record the depth in the data table.

8. Ask Dinosaur A to run across the soft sand or soil in a path that is parallel to his or her walking tracks. Observe the tracks made by running. Are they closer together or further apart than those made by walking? Are they deeper or more shallow than those made by walking? Make notes about the differences in tracks made by walking and running.

9. Repeat Steps 3–7 with Dinosaur B after raking the sand or soft soil clear of the tracks made by Dinosaur A.

Dinosaur Tracks, continued

Student	Height	Length of Stride	Length of Track	Depth of Track
Dinosaur A				
Dinosaur B				

Cleanup/Disposal

Follow your teacher's instructions for cleanup and disposal of materials.

Analysis

1. Which tracks were closest together, those of Dinosaur A or Dinosaur B?

_____

2. Which tracks were most shallow, those of Dinosaur A or Dinosaur B?

_____

Conclusions

1. You are a paleontologist studying the dinosaur tracks in Figure A. Look at Figure A. Which animal walked across the area first? Explain your answer.

_____

_____

2. Were all of the dinosaurs in Figure A the same size? Explain your answer.

_____

_____

3. Based on your observations, what story do these tracks tell you?

_____

_____

Explore Further

Work in groups of four or five to create tracks in soft soil for other groups to interpret.

Dinosaur Tracks, continued

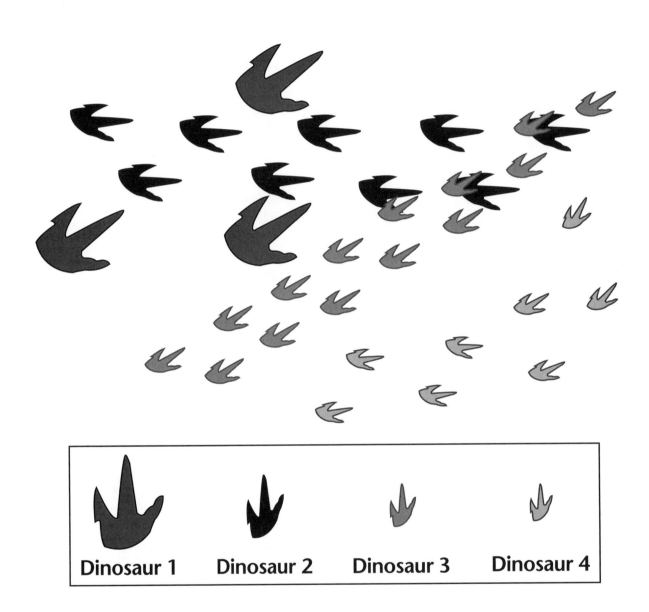

Figure A

Radioactive Dating

Radioactive dating is a method used to find the age of ancient objects. This technique is only possible in objects that contain radioactive elements. A radioactive element changes or decays into another substance, a daughter element. Radioactive decay takes place at a steady rate. Scientists can analyze the amount of radioactive element left in an object. They can compare it to the amount of daughter element present. By doing so, they can find the age of the object.

Ice is a material that changes states if exposed to temperatures below freezing. When temperature is constant, ice changes into water at a steady rate. You can compare the amount of ice in a sample to the amount of water in that sample over a period of time. This will help you find the rate at which ice melts. You can use this rate to determine the "age" of the ice.

In this lab, you will use a technique similar to radioactive dating to find the age of a material.

Materials   safety goggles   funnel
               lab coat or apron   graduated cylinder
               10 ice cubes   clock or watch
               2 large paper cups

Procedure

1. Put on safety goggles and a lab coat or apron.

2. Place 10 ice cubes in a paper cup.

3. Set the cup aside for 10 minutes.

4. After 10 minutes, pour the water that has collected in the cup into the graduated cylinder. Record the amount of water in the data table in the row labeled "10 minutes." **Safety Alert: Take care when working with glass.**

5. Set the cup of ice and graduated cylinder of water aside for 10 minutes.

6. After 10 minutes, add the water that has collected in the cup to the water in the graduated cylinder. Read the total volume and record this volume in the data table in the row labeled "20 minutes."

7. Repeat step 5 after 30 minutes and after 40 minutes.

Radioactive Dating, continued

Time	Total Amount of Water in Graduated Cylinder
0 minutes	**0**
10 minutes	
20 minutes	
30 minutes	
40 minutes	

Cleanup/Disposal

Follow your teacher's instructions for cleanup and disposal of materials.

Analysis

1. Where did the water in the cup come from?

_____

_____

2. What was the total volume of water collected after 10 minutes? _____ After 40 minutes? _____

Conclusions

1. What changes occur in a radioactive element over a period of time?

_____

_____

2. How is melting ice similar to the decay of a radioactive element?

_____

_____

3. How do scientists use radioactive dating to find the age of a fossil?

_____

_____

Explore Further

Find out how long a glass of partially melted ice has been melting.

Natural Selection in Action

Use with Investigation 13, pages 402–403

Mutations are random changes in DNA. Mutations create differences in the organisms. When the environment changes, some organisms can survive and reproduce due to changes from mutations. Natural selection may remove organisms without these characteristics. Then their genes are less likely to be passed on. In this investigation, you will demonstrate how a mutation affects the survival rate and reproduction of organisms in a certain environment.

Materials about 50 blue plastic chips
about 50 white plastic chips
blue pencil
red pencil

Procedure

1. Make a data table like the one shown below.

2. Scatter 12 white plastic chips and 12 blue plastic chips on your desktop. The white chips represent organisms that can survive in temperatures above 0°C. This is the normal temperature range for the species. The blue chips represent organisms of the same species with a mutation. The mutation allows them to survive in temperatures below 0°C and in the normal temperature range. These organisms are cold-tolerant. The desktop represents the environment for all the organisms. Record the number of blue chips, white chips, and total chips.

3. In the first event of this investigation, the temperature is above 0°C. To have the organisms reproduce, add a white chip or a blue chip for each pair of chips that are the same color. For example, in the first round of reproduction, you start with 12 white chips (6 pairs). Add 6 more white chips to the environment. You also have 12 blue chips (6 pairs). Add 6 more blue chips to the environment. Record the number of white chips, blue chips, and the total chips after this event.

4. Follow the directions and events described by your teacher. After each event, allow your organisms to reproduce as in Step 2.

5. Make a graph to compare the population growth of the white and blue organisms. Label the y-axis "Number of Organisms." Label the x-axis "Time" and mark off increments of 10,000 years. Use a blue pencil to track the population of the blue chips. Use a red pencil to track the population of the white chips.

Natural Selection in Action, continued

	Start	1st Event	2nd Event	3rd Event	4th Event	5th Event
blue						
white						
total						

Cleanup/Disposal

When you are finished, return the materials to your teacher.

Analysis

1. How was the number of normal-range organisms (white chips) affected by the cold weather?

_____

2. How was reproduction by both normal-range and cold-tolerant organisms affected by a colder climate?

_____

Conclusions

1. If the climate stays cold, what predictions can you make about the blue and white populations?

_____

_____

2. What would happen if the climate became warmer?

_____

3. What information is missing from this investigation?

_____

Explore Further

Try the simulation again introducing the missing element mentioned in Question 3.

Tracking Blood Type Alleles

Use with Discovery Investigation 13, pages 414–415

A person's blood type is determined by the inheritance of one of three alleles—A, B, or O—from each parent. The alleles together determine the blood type of that person. The allele combinations that create blood types are shown in the following table:

Blood Type	Allele Pairings	
A	AO	AA
B	BO	BB
O		OO
AB		AB

In this investigation, you will track alleles and blood types in a family. You will also examine how alleles are passed from parents to offspring.

Materials   Blood Type Allele Chart
coin

Procedure

1. Look at the Blood Type Allele Chart on the right. The chart represents three generations of a family. For each person, the top two squares show the person's blood type alleles. The bottom square shows the blood type that resulted from the combination of the two alleles.

2. Fill in the allele blanks for Child W and Child K. Determine each child's blood type.

3. Determine the blood types of Spouse W and Spouse K.

4. Choose which alleles will be passed from the second generation to the third generation. You may want to flip a coin to determine the allele a grandchild will receive.

5. Determine the blood types for all grandchildren.

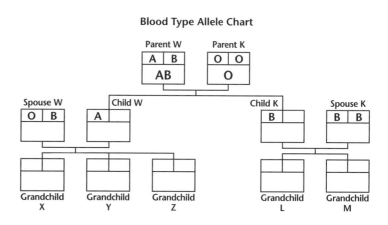

Blood Type Allele Chart

Tracking Blood Type Alleles, continued

Analysis

1. What blood types are possible for the grandchildren from Child W and Spouse W? Explain your answer.

_____

_____

2. What blood types are possible for the grandchildren from Child K and Spouse K? Explain your answer.

_____

_____

3. What allele was removed from the Child K–Spouse K branch to result in Grandchildren L and M?

_____

_____

Conclusions

1. What effect does the O allele have on determining blood type?

_____

_____

2. In this investigation, is it appropriate to use a coin flip to determine the alleles that are inherited? Explain your answer.

_____

_____

3. How could the offspring of Grandchild L or Grandchild M reclaim the lost allele?

_____

_____

Explore Further

A blood type also has a Rh factor. Parents pass on a positive Rh allele or a negative Rh allele. Go through the chart again and assign Rh alleles to all blood types.

Express Lab 14

Use with Express Lab 14, page 433

Materials   buttons or other objects

Procedure

1. Examine the buttons or other objects. Each object represents a different organism.

2. Working with a partner, develop a way to group these organisms into different "species."

3. When you are finished, be prepared to explain your method to your classmates.

Analysis

1. What are the unique characteristics of each species?

_____

_____

2. Which species are most closely related? How can you tell?

_____

_____

_____

3. List two or more additional characteristics that could be used to classify these organisms if they were actual living things.

_____

_____

_____

Magnetobacteria

Several types of bacteria are sensitive to the earth's magnetic field. In the Northern Hemisphere, the lines of force of the magnetic field curve downward as well as northward. Bacteria that can detect the field contain small granules of iron. Such organisms are known as magnetobacteria.

Magnetobacteria cannot survive in oxygen. They require an environment that has little or no oxygen. To avoid oxygen, they stay buried in soil or sediment.

If disturbed, magnetobacteria quickly orient with the earth's magnetic field. In the Northern Hemisphere, they swim along the lines of force toward the North Pole. Since these lines are curved, this path takes them northward and down into the sediments. In the Southern Hemisphere, they swim along a similar path toward the South Pole.

In this lab, you will observe the behavior of magnetobacteria.

Materials

safety goggles	compound microscope	glass slide
lab coat and apron	eyedropper	coverslip
about 1 cup of water and	bar magnet	petroleum jelly
sediment from a bay,	$\frac{1}{2}$ inch rubber O-ring	
marsh, lake, or pond		

Procedure

One week before the lab, collect about a cup of water and sediment from a bay, marsh, lake, or pond. Keep the sediment and water in an uncovered bowl in dim light. Over a week, the number of bacteria in the sample will increase.

1. Put on safety goggles and a lab coat or apron.

2. Coat one side of the O-ring with petroleum jelly. Place the O-ring on the glass slide.

3. Collect a sample of water and sediment with the eyedropper.

4. Place one drop of the sample on a coverslip.

5. Quickly turn the coverslip upside down so that the drop is hanging down.

6. Carefully place the coverslip and drop of sample on the O-ring. Make sure that the drop hangs freely in the center of the ring.

7. Position the slide on the microscope stage.

8. On low power, focus on the edge of the water drop. Switch microscope objectives and focus under 100X.

Magnetobacteria, continued

9. Look through the microscope. Hold the north end of the bar magnet near the edge that you are observing. Record your observations.

10. Set the magnet aside. Reposition the sample so that you can focus on another area.

11. Hold the south end of the bar magnet near the part of the sample that you are observing. Record your observations.

Cleanup/Disposal

Follow your teacher's instructions for cleanup and disposal of materials.

Analysis

1. What happened when the north end of the magnet was near the sample?

_____

2. What happened when the south end of the magnet was near the sample?

_____

Conclusions

1. Suggest a hypothesis that explains how the ability to move along the magnetic field helps these bacteria survive.

_____

_____

2. Would the ability to detect north be useful if these bacteria could not move? Explain your answer.

_____

_____

3. Some kinds of birds fly north each summer to mate and lay eggs. How might the ability to detect magnetic north help these organisms survive?

_____

_____

Explore Further

Test soil samples for other types of magnetobacteria.

Natural Selection in Bacteria

Use with Investigation 14, pages 438–439

People use antibiotics to destroy bacteria that can cause disease. Medicines, soaps, and other cleaners may contain antibiotics. Antibiotics kill bacteria or change their ability to reproduce or function. Through natural selection, some bacteria adapt and become resistant to antibiotics. This makes it more difficult to kill harmful bacteria with antibiotics. In this investigation, you will observe the effects of natural selection in bacteria.

Materials   safety goggles   2 nutrient agar petri   bacteria culture
                  lab coat or apron   dishes   forceps
                  gloves   Bunsen burner   antibiotic disk
                  wax pencil   inoculation loop

Procedure

1. Put on safety goggles, a lab coat or apron, and gloves.

2. Using a wax pencil, label the bottom of one petri dish A. Label the bottom of the other petri dish B. Write your name and the date on the bottom of each petri dish.

3. Follow your teacher's instructions to light the Bunsen burner.

4. To sterilize the inoculation loop, pass it through the flame. **Safety Alert: Be careful when working with an open flame.**

5. Collect a small amount of bacteria culture by putting the inoculation loop on the surface of the bacteria culture. With the inoculation loop, make a zigzag streak from top to bottom on the nutrient agar in petri dish A and petri dish B. Do not break the surface of the nutrient agar.

6. Using the forceps, pick up an antibiotic disk. Put the disk on petri dish A.

7. Cover both petri dishes. Put both petri dishes in a light- and temperature-controlled area as directed by your teacher.

8. Over the next three days, check your petri dishes every 24 hours. Record your observations.

Cleanup/Disposal

When you are finished, clean your lab area. Dispose of the used petri dishes according to your teacher's directions. Wash your hands well with soap and warm water.

Natural Selection in Bacteria, continued

Analysis

1. Compare the growth of the bacteria on petri dish A and petri dish B.

   _____

2. Describe the differences in the bacterial growth between your petri dish B and the petri dish B of other classmates. What factors cause these differences in growth?

   _____

   _____

Conclusions

1. What effect did the antibiotic disk have on the bacteria population on petri dish A?

   _____

2. What is occurring on petri dish A? What changes are occurring in the bacterial population as a result?

   _____

   _____

3. What problems can result by using antibiotics too often?

   _____

   _____

Explore Further

Take a sample of bacteria that is growing close to the antibiotic disk from petri dish A. Streak this sample onto a clean petri dish. Add an antibiotic disk. Cover the petri dish. Put this petri dish in a light-and temperature-controlled area as directed by your teacher. Check your dish every 24 hours over the next three days. Record your observations. Compare the growth of the bacteria on this petri dish with the growth on your petri dish A from the investigation. What could cause the differences in bacteria growth?

   _____

   _____

   _____

Plant Evolution

Use with Discovery Investigation 14, pages 445–446

The DNA of all life forms changes over generations. Many changes are slight and make little difference in the lives of the organisms. Environmental changes can cause organisms to change. Environmental changes allow some organisms with slight differences to grow and reproduce better than other organisms. Over time, these differences may cause new species to develop. In this investigation, you will examine several types of plants. You will determine how changes caused new species of plant life to develop.

Materials   safety goggles   fern plant
                 lab coat or apron   coniferous tree branch
                 moss plant   flowering tree branch

Procedure

1. Put on safety goggles and a lab coat or apron.

2. Examine the plants your teacher provided. Read the notes and descriptions that go with each plant.

3. In small groups, observe and discuss each plant. Record your observations. Your teacher will help guide your discussion and answer questions.

4. Use the notes provided by your teacher and your own observations to answer the Analysis questions.

Cleanup/Disposal

When you are finished, clean your lab area.

Analysis

1. What differences did you see between the moss and the other plants?

_____

Would each difference be an advantage or disadvantage? Explain your answer.

_____

_____

Plant Evolution, continued

2. How are the moss and the fern different from the other two plants?

_____

_____

3. The coniferous plant and the flowering plant are adapted to what kind of niche?

_____

4. What advantage does the flowering plant have compared to the other three plants?

_____

Why do you think this is an advantage?

_____

_____

Conclusions

Using your observations and the information provided, determine the order in which the four plants evolved. List the four plants, in order, from the earliest to the most recent.

_____

_____

_____

Explore Further

Research the physical and biological characteristics of blue-green algae. Do you think blue-green algae evolved sooner, the same time, or later compared to the four plants in this investigation? Explain your answer.

_____

_____

_____

Bird Adaptations

All birds have bills. The most important job of a bill is for feeding. A bill is designed to collect a bird's food. Since all birds do not eat the same food, bills come in hundreds of styles and shapes.

Within an area, the shapes of bills are determined by natural selection. Along coasts, where birds probe in the sand, long bills are more useful than short ones. In a pine forest, where birds chisel into trees to look for grubs, short, strong beaks are common.

In this lab, you will play the role of a bird. The shape of your bill will determine whether or not you survive.

Materials

safety goggles	straw	$\frac{1}{2}$ cup of birdseed
lab coat or apron	plastic fork	aluminum pie pan
chopsticks (1 set)	stopwatch or clock with	5 paper cups
tongs	a second hand	

Procedure

1. Put on safety goggles and a lab coat or apron.

2. Work in a group of four. Select the tool that you will use for your beak: a pair of chopsticks, tongs, a straw, or a plastic fork. Each member of the group should have one tool.

3. Spread about $\frac{1}{2}$ cup of birdseed in an aluminum pie pan. Place the aluminum pie pan on the desktop.

4. Practice using your tool to pick up bird seeds and put them in a paper cup.

5. After practicing, empty the cups of seeds back into the aluminum pie pan.

6. Use a clock or stopwatch as a timer. As a group, pick up seeds from the pie pan for 20 seconds.

7. At the end of 20 seconds, count the seeds in each cup. Record the totals in the data table on the line next to round 1. Do not return the seeds to the aluminum pie plate. Place them in another paper cup.

8. Any bird that collected less than 20 seeds "dies" and will not participate in round 2.

9. Repeat steps 5–7 for rounds 2, 3, 4, 5, and 6. After each round, count the number of seeds and record totals in the data table. After each round, eliminate "birds" that collect fewer than 20 seeds.

Bird Adaptations, continued

Number of Seeds Collected				
Round	Chopsticks	Tongs	Straw	Plastic Fork
round 1				
round 2				
round 3				
round 4				
round 5				
round 6				

Analysis

1. Which style of bird beak was best at collecting seeds? Why?

_____

2. Which style of bird beak was worst at collecting seeds? _____

Not all birds eat seeds. Some eat worms, insects, small mammals, and nectar in flowers. What kind of food might this style of beak been able to collect?

_____

Conclusions

1. What happens to animals that are not well-adapted for their environments?

_____

_____

2. How does natural selection determine the kinds of beaks that birds have?

_____

_____

3. How might a beak be shaped if a bird feeds on nectar in flower blossoms?

_____

_____

Explore Further

Experiment with other tools and find some that are very good at picking up bird seed. Research the beaks of birds to find out what kind of bird has a beak most like that tool.

Express Lab 15

Use with Express Lab 15, page 460

Materials   pictures of pets

Procedure

1. Bring to class a photograph, drawing, or magazine picture of a pet.

2. Using all of the pictures brought by your classmates, create your own classification system for the pets. Organize them in a way that makes sense. Create three or more different levels of organization.

3. Create an organizational chart for your classification system.

Analysis

1. On what features did you base your classification system?

_____

_____

_____

2. How is your classification system similar to the three-domain system? How is it different?

_____

_____

_____

Classifying Organisms

Use with Investigation 15, pages 462–463

Scientists classify all organisms by domain, kingdom, phylum or division, class, order, family, genus, and species. In this investigation, you will see that the more related organisms are, the higher the classification level they share.

Materials   pictures of different organisms

Procedure

1. Note the differences and similarities between the organisms in the pictures.

2. On a sheet of paper, make a classification chart. To start, list the three domains. Choose one organism from the pictures to represent each domain. List each organism next to its domain on your chart. Write a brief description of each organism and why it is classified in its domain.

3. Choose one organism from the pictures to represent each kingdom. List these on your classification chart. Write a brief description of each organism and why it is classified in its kingdom.

4. List the remaining organisms from the pictures on your chart.

Cleanup/Disposal

When you are finished, be sure your lab area is clean.

Analysis

1. What differences did you see in the sizes of the organisms in the three domains?

_____

_____

_____

2. Where are the organisms in each domain usually found?

_____

_____

_____

Classifying Organisms, continued

Conclusions

1. What features do scientists use to classify organisms into domains?

_____

_____

_____

2. What differences did you notice between organisms in different kingdoms?

_____

_____

_____

Explore Further

Say that you have discovered a new species. Make some notes about this new organism. Include its size, where it lives, and how and what it eats. Trade your information with a classmate. Decide how you would classify each other's organisms.

Lichens Up Close

Lichens grow on rocks and tree trunks. A lichen is recognized as a single living thing. However, it is made up of two or more different organisms. A lichen contains a fungus and one or more types of algae. The algae may be cyanobacteria, green algae, or both.

The organisms that make up a lichen depend on each other for survival. They cannot live independently. The fungus absorbs nutrients and water that it shares with the algae. The algae make food through photosynthesis and share it with the fungus.

In this lab, you will examine a lichen under the dissecting microscope.

Materials safety goggles   slide
              lab coat or apron   eyedropper
              scissors   water
              samples of several different notebook
                kinds of lichens   dissecting microscope
              forceps   colored pencils

Procedure

1. Put on safety goggles and a lab coat or apron.

2. Use scissors to snip off a small piece of lichen. **Safety Alert: Take care when working with scissors.**

3. Use forceps to place the piece of lichen on a slide. Use the eyedropper to add a few drops of water to the lichen.

4. Put the slide on the microscope stage. Focus on low power. Move the slide so that you can see all sections of the lichen.

5. Switch the focus to high power. Look closely at the cut edge of the lichen.

6. In your notebook, draw the lichen under high power. Use colored pencils to indicate the colors you see.

7. Remove the slide from the microscope. Repeat Steps 2 through 6 with another type of lichen.

Lichens Up Close, continued

Cleanup/Disposal

Follow your teacher's instructions for cleanup and disposal of materials.

Analysis

1. Under the microscope, some parts of the lichen are green. What makes up the green part of the lichen?

_____

2. Under the microscope, some parts of the lichen are gray or white. What makes up these parts of the lichen?

_____

Conclusions

1. Describe some of the ways in which lichens differ.

_____

_____

2. Do all lichens have the same amount of green material in them?   _____
Why do you think this is so?

_____

_____

3. Lichens often grow on dry surfaces like rocks and tree trunks. How do you think they survive in these places?

_____

_____

Explore Further

Examine pieces of lichen under the compound light microscope.

Earthworm Dissection

Earthworms are members of the phylum Annelida, segmented worms. An adult earthworm may have 100 or more segments. The inside of the body is divided by walls called septa.

Blood is pumped through an earthworm's body in vessels. Small masses of nerves near the mouth act as brains. Each mass is called a ganglion. Excretion is carried out by paired organs called nephridia. The digestive system is one long tube. It has a mouth at one end and an anus at the other end. Earthworms do not have lungs or gills for taking in oxygen. They exchange gases through their moist skin.

In this lab, you will dissect an earthworm and identify external and internal structures.

Materials

safety goggles	dissection tray	scalpel
lab coat or apron	dissecting needle	scissors
gloves	dissecting pins	probe
preserved earthworm	forceps	hand lens

Procedure

1. Put on safety goggles, a lab coat or apron, and gloves.

2. Put an earthworm in the dissecting tray. Identify the rounded, dorsal side. Locate the flat ventral side. Turn the worm so that the ventral side is up.

3. Locate the prostomium in Figure A. It is a lobe that extends over the mouth. Use a hand lens to find the prostomium on the worm.

4. Find the worm's clitellum, the swollen band that extends from segment 33 to segment 37. The clitellum produces an egg capsule. The capsule holds fertilized eggs until they mature.

5. Observe the hair-like setae with the hand lens. Setae are located on all segments except the first and last ones. They help the earthworm move.

6. Use the hand lens to view the ventral side of the worm. Refer to Figure A to identify the external parts of the reproductive system. Find the sperm grooves that extend from the clitellum to segment 15. Sperm are made in testes and pass out the genital pores. Genital pores are located on segments 15 and 26.

7. Find a pair of female genital pores on segment 14. Eggs made in the ovaries pass out through the female genital pores.

Earthworm Dissection, continued

8. Segment 10 holds two pairs of openings to the seminal receptacles. When worms mate, they swap sperm. Sperm from the donor travels along the sperm grooves to the seminal receptacles in the acceptor. These are tiny openings and may be difficult to find.

9. Turn the worm so that the dorsal side is up. Use the scalpels and scissors to make a shallow cut in the dorsal side of the clitellum. **Safety Alert: Take care when working with scissors and scalpels.**

10. Gently spread the incision open with the forceps. Inside the worm, separate each septum from the worm's organs with a dissecting needle.

11. Slowly continue the incision to segment 1. Separate the septa from the organs as you go. Pin down the sides of the worm with the dissecting pins.

12. Use Figure B to help you identify the worm's aortic arches. These act as hearts. Find the dorsal blood vessel, which runs the length of the body.

13. Find the digestive system. It is a long tube under the dorsal blood vessel. Earthworms take in soil and organic matter through the mouth. Material enters the pharynx then travels to the esophagus. The crop stores the food temporarily. The gizzard grinds food. After grinding, food travels to the intestines where nutrients are absorbed. Undigested material passes out through rectum and anus. Use Figure B to help you find the pharynx, esophagus, crop, gizzard, and intestine.

14. Locate the organs of the nervous system. Push aside the digestive and circulatory systems. The ventral nerve cord is a thin, gray strand. It runs from the head to the tail. Follow the cord toward the head. It connects to a nerve collar around the pharynx. Find one pair of ganglia under the pharynx. Locate another pair of ganglia above the pharynx. This second pair of ganglia serves as a brain.

15. Tiny nephridia, organs of excretion, are located in every segment. Refer to Figure B to identify some nephridia inside the body wall. Each one looks like a thin, white thread.

16. Push aside organs to locate the reproductive system. The large, yellowish seminal vesicles are part of the male system. Seminal vesicles store sperm. Very small testes are in segments 10 and 11.

17. Two pairs of yellowish seminal receptacles are located in segments 9 and 10. They are part of the female system. Seminal receptacles resemble seminal vesicles, but are smaller. Segment 13 holds a pair of ovaries. They are very small and difficult to see. Thin oviducts carry the eggs to female genital ducts in segment 14.

Cleanup/Disposal

Follow your teacher's instructions for cleanup and disposal of materials.

Earthworm Dissection, continued

Analysis

1. How is the earthworm's brain connected to the rest of its body?

_____

_____

2. Describe the excretory system of an earthworm.

_____

_____

3. How many pairs of aortic arches did you find? _____
How does the circulatory system of a worm differ from that of a human?

_____

_____

Conclusions

1. Where are the hair-like setae located? How do you think the setae help the earthworm survive?

_____

_____

_____

2. When two earthworms mate, they exchange sperm. Fertilization is external. Eggs are held
in cocoons until the young emerge. Since each worm produces eggs and sperm, why do
worms mate? If necessary, use reference material to help you find the answer.

_____

_____

_____

Explore Further

Remove and dissect the digestive system to find out what the earthworm has most recently eaten.

Figure A

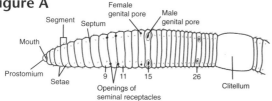

Figure B

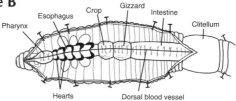

Using a Dichotomous Key

Use with Discovery Investigation 15, pages 495–496

To identify the species of an organism, scientists often use a dichotomous key. A dichotomous key allows the user to trace a path about the features of an organism. The user makes choices along the path based on observations about the organism. The dichotomous key splits into branches according to these choices until the user reaches the name of the organism. In this investigation, you will use a dichotomous key to identify the genus and species of several insects.

Materials   dichotomous key
                 specimens or photos of several insects

Procedure

1. Get a dichtomous key from your teacher.

2. Choose a specimen. Observe the specimen. **Safety Alert: Do not touch or harm the specimen.**

3. Look at the first branch of the dichtomous key. Determine which path to follow based on the features of your specimen.

4. Continue making observations and following the dichotomous key until you reach the name of the insect.

5. Use the dichotomous key to identify other specimens.

Cleanup/Disposal

When you are finished, be sure your lab area is clean.

Using a Dichotomous Key, continued

Analysis

1. What kinds of observations did you need to make to identify your specimens?

_____

_____

2. What type of information is used in a dichotomous key?

_____

3. What type of information is not used in a dichotomous key?

_____

Conclusions

1. To be effective, should a dichotomous key include descriptions of all organisms that could be identified? Explain your answer.

_____

_____

2. In Investigation 15, you used descriptions and names to classify organisms. How is using a dichotomous key more helpful than relying on descriptions and names?

_____

_____

Explore Further

Using objects in everyday life, create your own dichotomous key. For example, create a dichotomous key that identifies different cars. Test your dichotomous key by having someone identify one object.

Express Lab 16

Use with Express Lab 16, page 509

Materials   3 copies of a maze puzzle
stopwatch or clock with a second hand

Procedure

1. Work with a partner. Get a copy of a maze puzzle from your teacher.

2. Decide who will keep time and who will solve the maze puzzle. Time the person solving the puzzle. Stop timing the person when the puzzle is solved. Record this time.

3. Get another copy of the same maze puzzle. Have the same person solve the puzzle and the same person keep time. Record the time.

4. Get a third copy of the maze puzzle. Switch jobs with your partner.

Analysis

1. How did the time differ between the first attempt and the second attempt to solve the maze puzzle?

    _____

    What caused this difference?

    _____

2. How did the time in Step 4 compare to the first two times?

    _____

    What factors were different for the partner who solved the maze puzzle in Step 4?

    _____

3. Is the ability to solve the maze puzzle innate or learned?

    _____

    _____

Investigating Animal Behavior

Use with Investigation 16, pages 511–512

Animals often react when their environment changes. They adapt to the change or move to a more suitable environment. Sow bugs often live under rocks in gardens and yards. They eat decayed organic material. In this investigation, you will observe what type of environment sow bugs prefer.

Materials
safety goggles
lab coat or apron
shoebox and lid
scissors

6 paper towels
tap water
10 sow bugs
small lamp

Procedure

1. Put on goggles and a lab coat or apron.

2. Make half of your shoebox dark. Make the other half open to light. To do this, use scissors to remove half of the shoebox lid. **Safety Alert: Be careful when using scissors to cut the shoebox lid.**

3. Dampen the paper towels with tap water. Put a layer of damp paper towels in the entire bottom of the box.

4. Put the sow bugs in the middle of the box. **Safety Alert: Handle the sow bugs gently. Do not harm them.** Put the lid on the box. Half of the box should be dark and half should be exposed to the light. To make the exposed half lighter, shine a small lamp onto it. Be sure the lamp only lights up half of the box. Keep the other half dark.

5. Wait five minutes. Count how many sow bugs are in the light half and how many are in the dark half of your box. Record the numbers.

Cleanup/Disposal

After handling the sow bugs, wash your hands. Follow your teacher's instructions for collecting the sow bugs and disposal of material. When you are finished, be sure your lab area is clean.

Investigating Animal Behavior, continued

Analysis

1. In Step 5, how many sow bugs were in the light half of the box?   _____

How many were in the dark half?   _____

2. What was the stimulus in this investigation? Describe the behavior the sow bugs displayed in response to this stimulus.

_____

_____

Conclusions

1. What type of environment do sow bugs prefer?

_____

_____

2. Do you think the behavior of the sow bugs in this investigation is innate or learned?

_____

3. Why might sow bugs display this type of behavior?

_____

_____

Explore Further

Sow bugs are usually found in dark, damp environments. Design another investigation to determine whether sow bugs prefer a damp environment or a dry environment. Write a hypothesis. Have your procedure and Safety Alerts approved by your teacher. Conduct your investigation. Do your results support or refute your hypothesis?

Planarian Behavior

Planarians are flatworms and members of the phylum Platyhelminthes. They live in ponds and steams. The worms eat decaying meat. They avoid predators by hiding. Eyespots on the head help them stay out of well-lit areas where they could be seen.

Ethologists often use planarians to study behavior. The worms show many innate behaviors. They are also capable of learning new behaviors.

In this lab you will find out how a planarian reacts to an external stimulus.

Materials
    safety goggles
    lab coat or apron
    stopwatch
    20 cc syringe (without a needle)

    petri dish
    spring or pond water to fill petri dish
    planarian
    small paint brush

Procedure

1. Put on safety goggles and a lab coat or apron.

2. Work in groups of three. One person will hold the stopwatch and be the timer. One person will hold the syringe and be the tester. Another person will be the data recorder.

3. In a petri dish, put enough spring or pond water to cover the bottom.

4. Ask your teacher to transfer a planarian to your petri dish of water with a paint brush.

5. Let the planarian adapt to the petri dish for about five minutes.

6. In this experiment, you will observe the planarian's responses to puffs of air. Air puffs will be produced with the 20 cc syringe. When exposed to an air puff, a planarian may do nothing, contract, or turn away. The time between air puffs will 60 seconds.

7. Direct the plunger toward the head of the planarian. Depress the plunger to deliver an air puff. At the same time, turn on the stop watch.

8. Record the planarian's reaction to the air puff. Write "C" in the data table if the planarian contracts. Write "T" in the data table if the planarian turns away. Write "N" in the data table if the planarian does not respond.

9. Wait one minute. Then repeat Steps 7 and 8 until you have recorded 10 measurements.

Cleanup/Disposal

Follow your teacher's instructions for cleanup and disposal of materials.

Planarian Behavior, continued

Trial	Response of Planarian	Trial	Response of Planarian
1		6	
2		7	
3		8	
4		9	
5		10	

Analysis

1. What percentage of the time did the planarian turn when exposed to an air puff? _____
(To find percentage, add the number of times the planarian turned.
Divide this sum by 10. Multiply the quotient by 100.)

What percentage of the time did the planarian contract when exposed
to an air puff? _____

What percentage of the time did the planarian do nothing? _____

2. Compare your findings with the findings of other students. What are some of the reasons why

answers may be different? _____

_____

Conclusions

1. Many planarians turn to avoid air puffs. Do you think that this is learned or innate behavior?

_____ Why? _____

_____

2. How might your results differ if you tested the planarian 100 times rather than only 10 times?

_____

_____

3. What are some sources of error in this experiment?

_____

_____

Explore Further

Develop an experiment to find out if a planarian can be trained to avoid air puffs.

Exploring Human Communication

Use with Discovery Investigation 16, pages 527–528

People rely on spoken or written language to pass on information. They also use nonverbal methods to communicate. Some people may not realize that they use nonverbal communication. In this investigation, you will explore some ways humans communicate without using written or spoken language.

Materials   index cards

Procedure

1. In your group, discuss nonverbal ways animals and humans communicate. Examples are gestures, sounds, and body position. Record each example on an index card. Label the backs of the index cards Method.

2. Divide your group into two subgroups. One subgroup is the performers. The other subgroup is the audience.

3. In each subgroup, think of scenarios involving animal behavior. Examples are aggression and cooperation. Record each example on a card. Label the backs of the cards Scenario.

4. Have the performers select one of their scenario cards. Do not show the card to the audience.

5. Have the audience select an index card from the method pile. Put this card face up on the table so everyone can see it.

6. Have the performers act out the scenario using the communication method on the card. Have the audience interpret the scenario and discuss what clues made the communication successful.

7. Alternate between the performers and audiences to interpret scenarios. Continue until all the scenario cards are used. Replace the method card after each scenario so it can be reused.

Cleanup/Disposal

When you are finished, be sure your lab area is clean.

Exploring Human Communication, continued

Analysis

1. What clues led your subgroup to interpret the scenarios?

_____

_____

2. How do emotions play a part in communication?

_____

_____

Conclusions

1. What communication characteristics are associated with aggressive behavior, defensive behavior, and cooperative behavior?

_____

_____

2. Although people use spoken language to communicate ideas, words are only part of the communication. How do sounds and gestures communicate ideas? Give examples.

_____

_____

_____

Explore Further

Gestures, tones, and expressions may send a different message from the words humans use. Design another investigation in which some students make truthful statements and others make untruthful statements. Try to decide who is untruthful.

Crickets Are Territorial

Animals compete for resources such as food, mates, and nesting sites. Some animals physically guard their resources to protect them. This kind of behavior is called territoriality. A territory is an area used by an animal. Protecting a territory helps an animal survive and reproduce.

Adult male crickets are territorial. In this lab, you will find out how crickets defend their territory.

Materials   safety goggles   2 plastic cups   10 gallon aquarium
                 lab coat or apron   2 small pieces of   clock or watch
                 2 adult male crickets   aluminum foil   pencil

Procedure

1. Put on safety goggles and a lab coat or apron.

2. Remove 2 adult male crickets from the main holding tank. Adult crickets have wings. Examine the abdomens to identify males. Both males and females have two short spikes called abdominal cerci. A female also has an oviposter that extends between the two cerci. The oviposter is used to lay eggs.

3. Place each male in a plastic cup. Cover the two cups with aluminum foil. Carefully punch air holes in the foil with a pencil.

4. Put one covered cup in the 10 gallon aquarium. Remove the aluminum foil. Gently tip the cup so that the cricket leaves the cup. Wait 10 minutes to let the cricket get used to its surroundings. This cricket is the resident male.

5. Put the other male cricket into the aquarium. This cricket is the intruder. Put the intruder on the opposite side of the tank. Observe and record the behavior of the two crickets for 10 minutes. In your notebook, record how often each male:

   • chases the other cricket

   • fights with the other cricket

   • flees from the other cricket.

6. Keep count of the number of fights in the data table. Write the name of the winner and loser in the correct column. (A loser will try to escape. If one cricket loses three fights, end the experiment by removing the loser from the aquarium.)

Crickets Are Territorial, continued

Fight	Loser	Winner
1		
2		
3		
4		
5		

Cleanup/Disposal

Follow your teacher's instructions for cleanup and disposal of materials.

Analysis

1. How do crickets defend their territories?

_____

_____

2. Did the intruder try to avoid the resident?

_____

3. Where in the aquarium did the crickets interact?

_____

Conclusions

1. In this experiment, which cricket was dominant: the resident or the intruder? _____

How do you know? _____

2. In nature, how do you think male crickets defend their territories?

_____

_____

Explore Further

Exchange roles of the two crickets: Let the intruder play the role of resident.
See how the two crickets interact in the new roles.

Predators and Prey

Populations in an ecosystem interact. One type of interaction is predation. A predator is an animal that eats another species, the prey. Predation affects the size of a prey's population.

In this lab, you will simulate predation. The predators are snakes. Mice are the prey. You will graph changes in the populations of both the predators and prey.

Materials   200 squares of red construction paper, each about one inch
50 square of green construction paper, each about three inches by three inches
graph paper
red pencil
green pencil

Procedure

1. Your desktop represents an ecosystem. Red squares represent mice, which are prey. Green squares represent snakes, which are predators.

2. Toss three red squares on your desktop. In the data table, write 3 in the column "Number of Prey" for Generation 1.

3. Toss one green square on the desktop. In the data table, write 1 in the column "Number of Predators" for Generation 1.

4. A predator must have food to live. If the green square touches a red square, the predator eats the prey. In this experiment, if the predator does not eat prey, the predator dies.

   • If your green square is touching a red one, remove the red card. (Write 2 in the column "Number of Prey Remaining." Write 1 in the column "Number of Predators Remaining.")

   • If your green square is not touching a red one, remove the green card. (Write 3 under "Number of Prey Remaining." Write 0 under "Number of Predators Remaining.")

5. The number of prey doubles in each generation. In the data table, double the "Number of Prey Remaining" at the end of Generation 1. Add enough red cards to the desktop to equal that number.

6. If the predator did not capture prey, it died. A new predator takes it place in Generation 2. If the predator did capture prey, it survived. The number of surviving predators doubles each generation. If your predator survived, add another green card to the desktop.

Predators and Prey, continued

7. Repeat Steps 4 through 6 for a total of 20 generations. After each generation, add the correct number of red cards. Add or remove green cards as needed.

8. Graph the information on the data table. Put the number of generations on the *x*-axis. Place the population numbers for each generation (columns 2 and 3) on the *y*-axis. Plot "Number of Prey" in red pencil. Plot "Number of Predators" in green pencil.

Generations	Number of Prey	Number Predators Remaining	Number of Prey Remaining	Number Predators
1				
2				
3				
4				
5				
6				
7				
8				
9				
10				
11				
12				
13				
14				
15				
16				
17				
18				
19				
20				

Cleanup/Disposal

Follow your teacher's instructions for cleanup and disposal of materials.

Predators and Prey, continued

Analysis

1. As the number of prey increased, did the number of predators increase

   or decrease? _____

2. What would happen to the snake population if all of the mice died of disease?

   _____

3. What would happen to mouse populations if snakes were not present?

   _____

   _____

Conclusions

1. In well-established communities, the populations of predators and prey stay about
   the same. Why is this true?

   _____

   _____

2. Owls are predators of mice and snakes. How do the populations of mice and snakes
   change if owls join the community?

   _____

   _____

Explore Further

   Repeat the experiment with owls added to the community.

Express Lab 17

Use with Express Lab 17, page 544

Materials   6 index cards
six-sided number cube
30 buttons

Procedure

1. With a pen, label the index cards from 1 to 6.

2. Make a rectangle with two rows of index cards. In row 1, lay out index cards 1 to 3. In row 2, lay out index cards 4 to 6. The rectangle represents an ecosystem.

3. Each button represents one organism in a population. Select a distribution pattern: uniform, clumped, or random.

4. Put the buttons on the rectangle to show the distribution pattern you selected.

5. Roll the number cube. Find the card with that number. The organisms on this index card represent your sample.

Analysis

1. Does your sample contain one-sixth of the organisms in your ecosystem? Explain your answer.

_____

_____

2. How do distribution patterns affect sampling?

_____

_____

3. Which pattern will give the best estimate of true population size?

_____

Estimating Population Size

Use with Investigation 17, pages 546–547

To study a population, ecologists must determine its size. Ecologists usually cannot count all the members of a population. Instead, they use sampling methods to estimate the size of a population. In this investigation, you will use the mark-recapture sampling method to estimate the size of a population of navy beans. Ecologists often use the mark-recapture method to estimate the size of animal populations.

Materials   small paper bag containing dried navy beans
red wax pencil

Procedure

1. Remove 10 beans from the bag. Use the red wax pencil to put a large dot on each of the 10 navy beans. **Safety Alert: Do not put the navy beans in or near your mouth.**

2. Return the marked navy beans to the paper bag. Close the bag. Shake the bag gently.

3. Remove 20 navy beans from the bag. This is your sample. Count the number of navy beans with red dots. The navy beans with red dots are your marked recaptures. Record this number.

4. Return the navy beans with red dots to the bag.

5. Count the total number of navy beans in the bag. This is the actual population size. Record this number.

Analysis

1. What does each navy bean represent?

_____

2. What does the bag represent?

_____

Estimating Population Size, continued

3. Use the following equation to estimate the population size, N: $N = \dfrac{M \times S}{R}$

   Where   **M** = number marked

           S = total number in the sample

           R = number of marked recaptured

   Estimation: _____

   How close was your estimate of the population size to the total number of navy beans in the bag?

   _____

   _____

Cleanup/Disposal

Follow your teacher's instructions for cleanup and disposal of materials.

Conclusions

1. The mark-recapture method assumes that each marked individual has the same chance of being recaptured as each unmarked individual. What problems do you see with this assumption?

   _____

   _____

   _____

2. In a real population, what are some events or factors that could affect the accuracy of the mark-recapture method?

   _____

   _____

3. Write a new question about estimating population size that you could explore in another investigation.

   _____

   _____

Explore Further

Use a similar procedure to explore the effect of sample size on estimating population size.

Surveying an Ecological Community

Use with Discovery Investigation 17, pages 553–554

An ecological community is made of all the biotic, or living, species in an ecosystem. Ecology is the study of the interactions among living things and the nonliving things in an environment. Living things are the biotic factors in the environment. Abiotic factors are nonliving things, such as air, temperature, light, and water. In this investigation, you will survey an ecological community in your area.

Materials   heavy gloves
meterstick
4 wood stakes
string
green, blue, brown, black, orange pencils or markers

Procedure

1. Put on heavy gloves.

2. Using a meterstick, measure a 5 meter by 5 meter site. Put a stake at each corner of the site. **Safety Alert: Wear heavy gloves to push the stake into the ground. Stay only in the area as directed by your teacher.**

3. Make a border around the site by looping string around the first stake. Continue looping string around each stake until you have formed a border around the site.

4. To map your site, draw a 15 centimeter by 15 centimeter square on a sheet of paper. Draw the physical features of your site on your map.

5. Use a green pencil or marker to draw the plants in your site. Use blue to draw the animals. Use brown to represent evidence of animals, such as egg cases, animal tracks, or burrows. Use black to show dead organisms or parts of organisms, such as fallen leaves or twigs. Use orange to show decomposers.

6. Write a hypothesis, Safety Alerts, and procedure describing how to determine which organism in your site has the greatest population density.

7. Have your hypothesis, Safety Alerts, and procedure approved by your teacher. Carry out your experiment.

Cleanup/Disposal

Follow your teacher's instructions for cleanup and disposal of materials.

Surveying an Ecological Community, continued

Analysis

1. List the abiotic and biotic features of your site.

_____

_____

2. Describe a distribution pattern—uniform, clumped, or random—for one organism in your site.

_____

_____

3. Which organisms at your site are producers? Which organisms are consumers?

_____

_____

4. Describe evidence of primary succession at your site.

_____

_____

Conclusions

1. Was your hypothesis supported by the results of your investigation? _____

2. Are consumers or producers found in the greatest number at your site? _____

3. What density-dependent and density-independent factors are likely to affect the organisms at your site?

_____

_____

Explore Further

What relationships exist among two or more different kinds of organisms at your site? Suggest a procedure to answer this question.

Owl Pellets

Owls are predators. They swallow their prey whole. Undigestible body parts of prey are regurgitated in pellets. Pellets reflect an owl's diet. They also indicate the kinds of organisms that live the in the owl's habitat.

In this lab, you will dissect an owl pellet. The pellets used in lab have been fumigated to kill bacteria.

Materials
safety goggles
lab coat or apron
owl pellet
small bowl of water
probe
forceps
newspaper

Procedure

1. Put on safety goggles and a lab coat or apron.

2. Gently twist the owl pellet to separate it into two or three pieces. Take care not to break any bones in the pellet.

3. Use forceps to pick up one piece of the pellet. Dip the piece in a bowl of water. Deposit the wet piece of pellet on the newspaper. Use forceps, a probe, and your fingers to remove the bones from the pellet. **Safety Alert: Take care when working with sharp instruments.**

4. Remove all of the bones from each piece of the owl pellet.

5. Search the Internet or the library for pictures of the skeletons of birds, mice, shrew, and moles. On the Internet, use the search words "owl pellet lab."

6. Using your research material as a guide, separate the bones by type: skulls and jaws, ribs, vertebrae, hips and shoulders, feet and toe bones, and legs.

Cleanup/Disposal

Follow your teacher's instructions for cleanup and disposal of materials.

Owl Pellets, continued

Analysis

1. How many animals were in your owl pellet? _____ How do you know?

_____

2. What was the primary food for your owl?

_____

Conclusions

1. Assume that your owl regurgitates one pellet each day. How many animals would

your owl eat in a year? _____

2. How would populations of prey animals change if owls were removed from community?

_____

_____

3. From the objects you found in the owl pellet, what do you know about the owl's
digestive system?

_____

_____

Explore Further

Assemble one of the skeletons of prey animals found in the owl pellet.

Express Lab 18

Use with Express Lab 18, page 570

Materials   3 index cards
marker
photographs of organisms

Procedure

1. Label one index card "P" for producer. Label a second index card "C " for consumer. Label a third index card "D" for decomposers.

2. Put the cards in a row. Put each photograph under the correct index card to show the role the organism plays in its ecosystem. Some organisms may play more than one role.

Analysis

1. Which organisms are producers?

   _____

   Which are consumers?

   _____

   Which are decomposers?

   _____

2. Why is each trophic level necessary in an ecosystem?

   _____

   _____

Building a Food Web

Use with Investigation 18, pages 571–572

Ecologists observe the feeding relationships among organisms to study how energy moves through an ecosystem. In this investigation, you will build a food chain. The food chain will show a sequence, or series, of feeding relationships. You will then combine your food chain with other food chains to build a food web.

Materials   organism cards

Procedure

1. Your teacher will give you a set of organism cards. Separate the cards into three groups to represent each trophic level: producers, consumers, and decomposers.

2. Begin your food chain by putting a producer card at the lower edge of your desktop.

3. Put a consumer card just above the producer card. A consumer eats a producer. Put the other consumer cards on your desktop in the correct sequence.

4. Add one or more decomposer cards to complete your food chain. Copy your food chain on a sheet of paper.

5. Combine your food chain cards with those of a classmate. Use your knowledge of trophic structure to arrange the cards into a food web. On a sheet of paper, copy your food chain.

Analysis

1. How was your food chain similar to your classmate's?

_____

_____

How was it different?

_____

_____

2. What is the difference between a food chain and a food web?

_____

_____

Building a Food Web, continued

Conclusions

1. What would happen to your food chain if sunlight no longer existed? Explain your answer.

   _____

   _____

2. Write a new question about the role of each trophic level you could explore in another Investigation.

   _____

   _____

Explore Further

Use the procedure above to discuss the differences in the numbers of individuals at each trophic level.

_____

_____

_____

Phosphate in Aquatic Ecosystems

Use with Discovery Investigation 18, pages 578–579

Phosphorus is an element needed by organisms. In most ecosystems, phosphorus occurs in the form of phosphate, which can be found in soil and rocks. Too little phosphate can limit plant growth.

Materials safety goggles
      lab coat or apron
      gallon glass jar
      pond water
      pond plants, such as *Elodea*
      pond animals, such as protozoa or *Daphnia*
      four 250 mL beakers
      high-phosphate detergent solution
      eyedropper

Procedure

1. Put on safety goggles and a lab coat or apron.

2. Fill the glass jar half-full with pond water.

3. Add the pond plants and animals to the water.

4. Put the glass jar on a sunny windowsill for several days.

5. When the water in the glass jar has begun to turn green, divide the pond water and plants equally among the four beakers. Each beaker will represent an aquatic ecosystem. **Safety Alert: Be sure to wash your hands immediately after handling the pond water.**

6. Write a hypothesis and procedure describing how you can determine the effects of phosphate on aquatic ecosystems.

7. Have your hypothesis, procedure, and Safety Alerts approved by your teacher.

8. Set up your experiment. Observe and record your results after several days.

Phosphate in Aquatic Ecosystems, continued

Analysis

1. Describe the appearance of each beaker after several days.

_____

_____

_____

2. List the independent variable and the dependent variable in your experiment.

_____

_____

_____

Conclusions

1. What is the effect of adding phosphate to aquatic ecosystems?

_____

_____

_____

2. Why do you think many states have banned phosphates from household laundry detergents?

_____

_____

Explore Further

What will eventually happen to the plants and animals in an aquatic ecosystem that contains a lot of phosphate? Suggest a procedure to answer this question.

_____

_____

_____

_____

Mini Ecosystem

In ecosystems, living things interact with the nonliving environment. Ecosystems are found in all parts of the world. Each type of ecosystem is unique. Forest ecosystems may be home to plants like ferns, trees, and shrubs. The animals there might include squirrels, birds, and deer. In a desert ecosystem, the plants may be cacti and yucca. Lizards, snakes, and birds are some of the animals that live in deserts.

In this lab, you will create a mini ecosystem similar to the ecosystem where you live.

Materials

safety goggles
lab coat or apron
10 gallon aquarium with a perforated
   cover or a wide-mouth, glass gallon
   jar with a perforated lid
2 cups gravel
4 cups soil from a local ecosystem

a few small plants from a local ecosystem
$\frac{1}{2}$ cup water
small beaker or cup
a few small animals from a local ecosystem
   such as worms or crickets
tap water
ruler

Procedure

1. Put on safety goggles and a lab coat or apron.

2. Spread about $\frac{1}{2}$ inch of gravel in the bottom of the aquarium. If you are using a wide-mouth gallon jar, turn the jar on its side before spreading the gravel.

3. Put a layer of soil on top of the gravel. Spread the soil so that it is two or three inches deep.

4. Several kinds of animals and plants are available. They have been collected from an ecosystem near you. Plant two or three different kinds of plants in your mini ecosystem.

5. Use the small beaker or cup to water the plants. Add just enough water to dampen the soil. Do not create puddles.

6. Gently transfer two or three animals to your mini ecosystem.

7. Put a cover or lid on the mini ecosystem.

8. Situate the mini ecosystem so it receives indirect sunlight.

9. Check on the mini ecosystem every day for 2 weeks. Add water if needed. Keep a daily log of activity and changes.

Cleanup/Disposal

Follow your teacher's instructions for cleanup and disposal of materials.

Mini Ecosystem, continued

Analysis

1. Name and describe the plants in your ecosystem.

   _____

   _____

2. Name and describe the animals in your ecosystem.

   _____

   _____

Conclusions

1. Did your mini ecosystem change over the two week period?   _____
   If so, describe the changes.

   _____

   _____

2. What is the job of the plants in your ecosystem?

   _____

   _____

   Predict what would happen if you removed these plants.

   _____

   _____

3. Pretend that NASA will send people to live on the moon for a year. It is your job to design
   an artificial ecosystem for these people. Describe the system you would recommend.

   _____

   _____

   _____

   _____

   _____

Explore Further

Create different types of mini ecosystems such as forests, deserts, ponds, or grasslands.

Effects of Light

Sunlight is the source of energy for living things on the earth. In ecosystems, energy moves from one living thing to another. Plants capture energy from the sun. When animals eat the plants, they take in energy. Decomposers get energy by consuming dead plants and animals.

In this lab, you will find out what happens when an ecosystem cannot get sunlight.

Materials   safety goggles
lab coat or apron
meterstick, stakes, and string
magnifying glass
black plastic trash bags
3 or 4 small rocks

Procedure

1. Put on safety goggles and a lab coat or apron.

2. Select a small outdoor area that is part of an ecosystem. You will observe this area for two weeks.

3. Using a meterstick, measure an area that is one meter square. Mark the area with string and stakes.

4. Create a data table in your notebook like the one below. Use it to record information about the sample area.

	Plants (number of type, color of plants)	**Animals** (number of each type)
Day 1		
Day 7		
Day 14		

Effects of Light, continued

5. Cover the sample area with black trash bags. Secure the bags in place with rocks.

6. After seven days, check the sample area again. In the data table, update the condition of the plants and animals.

7. Check the sample area again after fourteen days. In the data table, update the condition of plants and animals.

Cleanup/Disposal

Follow your teacher's instructions for cleanup and disposal of materials.

Analysis

1. What kinds of plants live in the sample area?

_____

_____

2. What kinds of animals live in the sample area?

_____

_____

Conclusions

1. How did the condition of the plants change over the two weeks?

_____

_____

2. Did the number of animals change over the two weeks?

_____

_____

3. What is the role of the sun in an ecosystem?

_____

_____

Explore Further

Carry out this experiment indoors using mini ecosystems.

Express Lab 19

Use with Express Lab 19, page 597

Materials   rainwater sample
small jar with lid
forceps
2 pieces of pH paper
2 eyedroppers
pH chart
distilled water

Procedure

1. In a small jar, collect a small sample of rainwater from a clean puddle or directly from the air. Put the lid on the jar and bring it to class.

2. Put on safety goggles and a lab coat or apron.

3. Use the forceps to pick up a piece of pH paper. Use an eyedropper to put a drop of distilled water onto the pH paper.

4. Compare the color of the wet pH paper to the pH chart. Record your observations.

5. Using a new eyedropper, repeat Steps 3 and 4 with a drop of rainwater.

6. When you are finished, wash your hands well.

Analysis

1. What is the pH of distilled water?   _____

2. What is the pH of the rainwater? Is this acid rain?   _____

Measuring Particulates in the Air

Use with Investigation 19, pages 599–600

Particulates are a form of air pollution. They are tiny particles suspended in the air you breathe. Particulates come from fires, tobacco smoke, vehicle exhaust, plants, and animals. In this investigation, you will collect two air samples and count the particulates in each sample. Where do you think you will find the most particulates?

Materials

safety goggles	marker
lab coat or apron	petroleum jelly
2 microscope slides	2 petri dish lids
2 petri dishes	microscope

Procedure

1. Put on safety goggles and a lab coat or apron.

2. Make a data table like the one shown below.

3. Get two microscope slides and two petri dishes with lids. Using a marker, label a corner of one slide A. Label a corner of the other slide B. **Safety Alert: Handle glass microscope slides with care. Dispose of broken glass properly.**

4. Choose two locations to test for particulates. Using a marker, label the bottom of a petri dish A. Write its location. Label the bottom of the other petri dish B. Write its location.

	Slide A	Slide B
Location		
Number of particulates— first field of view		
Second field of view		
Third field of view		
Fourth field of view		
Fifth field of view		
Total number of particulates		

5. Use petroleum jelly to lightly coat the unlabeled side of each slide. Put the slide, with the petroleum jelly side up, in the petri dish with the same letter. Wash your hands well.

Measuring Particulates in the Air, continued

6. Put the uncovered petri dishes containing the slides in the chosen locations. Do not disturb them for 24 hours.

7. Cover the petri dishes with the lids.

8. Use a microscope to observe slide A. Use low power and then high power. Count the number of particulates in each of 5 different high-power fields of view. Record your data. Find the total number of particulates counted for slide A.

9. Repeat Step 8 for slide B.

Cleanup/Disposal

When you are finished, wash the slides and petri dishes thoroughly with detergent and warm water. Wash your hands well.

Analysis

1. What is the purpose of the petroleum jelly?

_____

2. Make a graph comparing the total number of particulates counted from your two locations. What kind of graph would best compare your data?

_____

Conclusions

1. Which location had the largest number of particulates? _____

2. Where do you think the particulates in your locations came from?

_____

_____

3. Write a new question about particulates that you could explore in another investigation.

_____

_____

Explore Further

If you know someone who smokes, repeat the investigation by placing a slide in his or her home. Place a slide in the home of a nonsmoker for comparison.

Greenhouse Gases

Carbon dioxide and other gases form a layer in the atmosphere. The layer acts as a barrier. Like glass in a greenhouse, the barrier traps the sun's heat. The gases in this layer are called greenhouses gases. They are a normal part of the atmosphere. Thanks to greenhouses gases, the earth's surface is warm.

Emissions from cars and factories have added additional carbon dioxide to the atmosphere. This carbon dioxide makes the layer of greenhouse gases thicker than normal. As a result, the earth's surface is warmer than it was in the past.

In this lab, you will find out how a barrier can trap heat.

Materials
    safety goggles   2 labels
    lab coat or apron   plastic wrap
    wax pencil   clock or watch
    2 beakers or jars   sunny area or sun lamp
    2 small thermometers

Procedure

1. Put on safety goggles and a lab coat or apron.

2. Make a data table like the one below.

Temperature	Beaker A	Beaker B
Beginning		
After 5 minutes		
After 10 minutes		

3. Using a wax pencil, label one beaker A. Label the other beaker B.

4. Place a thermometer in each beaker.

5. Wait 5 minutes. Read the temperature on each thermometer. Record the temperatures in the data table in the row labeled Beginning.

6. Cover Beaker B with plastic wrap. Make a tight seal around the top of the beaker.

7. Place both beakers in a sunny area or under a sunlamp.

Greenhouse Gases, continued

8. Wait 5 minutes. Read the temperature in each beaker. Record the temperature in the row labeled "After 5 minutes."

9. After 10 minutes, read the temperature in each beaker. Record the temperature in the row labeled "After 10 minutes."

Cleanup/Disposal

Follow your teacher's instructions for cleanup and disposal of materials.

Analysis

1. How much did the temperature change in Beaker A?   _____

How much did it change in Beaker B?   _____

2. In this experiment, what material represents the greenhouse gases?   _____

Conclusions

1. How does plastic wrap affect the temperature in a beaker?

_____

_____

2. How do greenhouse gases affect the temperature on the earth?

_____

_____

3. What are some of the effects of excess greenhouse gases?

_____

_____

Explore Further

Compare results of this experiment on a cloudy day and on a sunny day.

Conservation of Soil

Use with Discovery Investigation 19, pages 611–612

One of the most important natural resources is soil. Soil provides nutrients to plants. Plants are the base of almost all food chains on the earth. In this investigation, you will compare the effect of running water on the soil of a bare slope and on a slope planted with grass. What causes soil erosion? What happens to a bare slope and a grassy slope during a rainstorm? How can soil be conserved? You will investigate these questions.

Materials

2 small aluminum pans, each
  with 6 holes punched in one end
garden soil
large aluminum pan
turf to fit in a small aluminum pan
watering can

graduated cylinder or
  metric measuring cup
water
2 or 3 books or wooden boards
  to raise end of pan

Procedure

1. Discuss the questions in the first paragraph with your group. Write a hypothesis to answer this question: How does planting a slope with grass affect the amount of soil erosion caused by a rainstorm? The hypothesis should be one you can test.

2. Design an experiment to test your hypothesis. Make a table for the data you will collect. **Safety Alert: Be sure to include any Safety Alerts such as protecting your clothing and not touching your mouth or eyes with your hands.**

3. Have your hypothesis, Safety Alerts, experimental design, and data table approved by your teacher.

4. Carry out your experiment.

Cleanup/Disposal

When you are finished, clean up your materials and wash your hands with warm, soapy water.

Conservation of Soil, continued

Analysis

1. How much water ran off the bare slope? What did the water look like?

_____

_____

2. How much water ran off the slope with turf? What did the water look like?

_____

_____

Conclusions

1. Was your hypothesis supported by the results of your experiment?   _____

2. How does this experiment model soil erosion?

_____

_____

_____

3. How could a farmer practice soil conservation?

_____

_____

_____

Explore Further

Design an experiment to determine how the steepness of a slope affects erosion.
Carry out the experiment. Record your results.

Overpackaging

Americans enjoy products that are convenient. Many products are sold in disposable packaging. Packaging poses problems for the environment. It ends up in trash cans and landfills. One-third of trash is material used for packaging. Packaging is one reason that landfills are overcrowded. In addition, the manufacture of packaging contributes to pollution and uses energy.

In this lab, you will compare the amount of packaging in different size bags of potato chips.

Materials   safety goggles   calculator   ruler
           lab coat or apron   single serving bag of   large bag of potato chips
           scissors   potato chips   small bowl
           large bowl

Procedure

1. Put on safety goggles and a lab coat or apron.

2. Create a data table like the one below.

	Large bag	**Single Serving Bag**
Number of potato chips in package		
Area of packaging	_____ square inches	_____ square inches
Chips per square inch of packaging	_____ chips/ square inch	_____ chips/ square inch

3. Using scissors, cut open the large package of potato chips. Pour the contents of the package into the large bowl.

4. Count the number of potato chips in the package. Record that number in the first row of the data table.

5. Flatten the potato chip package. Using a ruler, measure the length and width of the package. Record these measurements in your notebook.

6. Multiply the length times the width. The product is the area of one side of the bag. This area is one-half of the packaging in the bag.

7. Find the total area of the potato chip bag. Multiply the area of one side of the potato chip package by two. Record your answer in the second row of the data table.

Overpackaging, continued

8. Find the number of potato chips per square inch of packaging. To do this, divide the number of potato chips into the area of the package. Record your answer in the third row of the data table.

9. Repeat Steps 3–7 for the single serving bag of potato chips. Use a small bowl.

Cleanup/Disposal

Follow your teacher's instructions for cleanup and disposal of materials.

Analysis

1. In the big package, how many potato chips are packed in one square inch of packaging material?   _____

   In the small package, how many potato chips are packed in one square inch of packaging?   _____

2. Which package uses the least amount of material per chip?

   _____

   _____

Conclusions

1. What happens to empty potato chip bags?

   _____

   _____

2. List other foods that are sold in single serving and large sizes.

   _____

   _____

3. How could a grocery shopper help reduce trash?

   _____

   _____

Explore Further

Write a letter to a manufacturer to suggest ways to reduce packaging. Write another letter to the editor of a local newspaper. Explain how citizens can reduce the amount of trash they produce.